JEWS AND BLACKS

JEWS AND BLACKS

The Classic American Minorities

BEN HALPERN

HERDER AND HERDER

1971
HERDER AND HERDER NEW YORK
232 Madison Avenue, New York 10016

Library of Congress Catalog Card Number: 70–146300
© 1971 by Herder and Herder, Inc.
Manufaceured in the United States

Contents

*To Elkan and Judy
and Joe and Joan
across the generation gap*

JEWS AND BLACKS

I. A View from Waltham

WALTHAM in itself means little on the American national scene. It is a small urban wasteland on the outskirts of Boston, a town only recently lifted from deep depression by the mysterious science-related industries of Route 128, growing wild like marijuana on its outer fringe. The people of Waltham, middle Americans in a very modest way, are bemused and disquieted and quite often annoyed by the newcomers and new manners encroaching upon their turf.

Incongruously perched like a flock of brassy bantam roosters upon a clutch of hills in this grey and dreary town stand, or spring up, the brick, concrete, and wide-glass buildings of Brandeis: a "nonsectarian Jewish-sponsored university" come to roost in a workers' and lower-middle class, mainly Catholic, community where high school seniors lose face if they talk of going to college. Brandeis belongs to the Boston of Harvard and MIT and ties in to the main American powerhouses of New York and Washington. But above all it belongs to the New York Jewish intellectual establishment: to *Partisan Review, Dissent, Commentary,* and *The New York Review of Books;* to the literary, theatrical, art, and musical avant-garde and to the pale pink to deep-dyed red spectrum of liberal, left liberal, and radical politics.

Perhaps half of the Brandeis faculty are Jews. Most of them make little or nothing of the fact and prefer not to notice their high ethnic concentration. The Gentile half of the professional and instructional staff includes, on the other hand, many who

11

are in Brandeis partly because they are attracted by the loose and lively, and sometimes high-pitched, nominally Jewish host society. As for the students of Brandeis—as New Left in life-style as the faculty is Old Left—they are Jews in considerably higher proportion; but this result is not produced by choice of the admissions officers. Tacitly preferential policies from the beginning favored a more heterogeneous mix, but had only relatively minor success in attracting bright young Catholics from the Boston area. More recently the general countrywide pressure for openly preferential admission quotas for black students brought a significant proportion of young Negroes to the campus—and the explicit character of the preference also raised serious controversial issues.

This is the local perspective from which these remarks on the changing Jewish-black relationship in America are written. But a view depends as much, or more, on the viewer's personal perspective as on the observation point from which he sets his sights. This is not "*the* view from Waltham" but "*a* view from Waltham," and, no doubt, a rather eccentric view, both for Waltham and for Brandeis-in-Waltham.

These notes and comments are those of a committed, not a nominal Jew; but of a Jew whose commitment is to the turn-of-the-century secular, nationalist, socialist-Zionist Jewishness of the Eastern European 1905 generation, and not to the churchly Judaism of today's older, established American Jews nor to the younger, contemporary Jews' problematic Jewish-identity quest. They are, and are not, the views of a professional teacher at Brandeis; for they represent a current summary of observations initially made in the midst of a life of professional Zionist activism and now complemented and revised in the quasi-retirement of the academy. The personal perspective is obviously still rooted in the active part of my life. To what extent it also reflects academic values, either out of an inherent affinity for them or the influence of a long association, I shall leave the reader to judge.

12

All current discussion of black Americans—but not of American Jews—raises radical questions about the nominally liberal principles of America. The personal perspective of my own comments has, from their first statement to the present, always involved radical questions about nominally liberal principles relating to American Jews. This suggests similarities to the current black critique of America; but it also, of course, involves significant differences.

ALIKE OR DIFFERENT?

Styles seem to change as rapidly these days in conventions of thought as in women's dress. Not more than a decade ago there would be no question about the proper opening for a discussion of Jews, Negroes, and the relations between them. Both were clearly the classic unassimilated, and possibly unassimilable, minorities in America. They were both exceptions to the rule that America *had* no minorities.

Because of this, it was not in the best of taste to talk much in terms of their actual situation. Apart from Jewish and Negro nationalists, of whom there were few able to command attention, only right-wing bigots harped on the unbridgeable difference from other Americans which Jews and Negroes had in common. Respectable Americans dwelt on the abstract principles (rather than concrete reforms) that would, gradually but surely, integrate these Americans fully in a homogeneous greater society.

Still less did most observers concern themselves with the different conditions that held up rapid assimilation of Jews and Negroes, though such differences were obvious. The invisible barrier to the absorption of the Jews was quite clearly religion, their own or that of the Gentiles; while the Negroes were kept apart by the visible barrier of color. This difference, or other differences between them, might interest parochial-minded Jews or Negroes, but hardly anyone else. If others men-

13

tioned Jews and Negroes in the same breath, it was to pick away at the nagging issue the two raised in common: why both together were and, it looked like, were remaining, unabsorbed in the homogenized mass of Americans; why both alike were so intractably different.

This is not the current tone of comment on Jews, Negroes, or the relations between them. For one thing, if both were conceived today to be irreducibly different from the standard American, it would not be regarded by the more advanced thinkers as a problem at all, but as a most promising beginning. It is axiomatic for many that all standards of the past generation have to be scrapped; or, if you please, they need revaluation. The old are morally bankrupt, and all hope rests in the young. The declining West has collapsed, and, for that matter, so has the superpower of the East. The future looks to the Third World for light. To be different from the establishment is the beginning of virtue.

In such a climate of discussion, all differences, including differences between Jews and Negroes, become a matter of general significance and of more than parochial interest. The more militant black nationalists are in no doubt at all about where Jews belong. They are in no way different from any other part of the establishment. They are whites, part of the honky majority, standard lily-white Americans who can have nothing in common with the black revolution. Some blacks more recently are willing to join Jews of the New Left in a revolutionary united front whose bond of union is none other than anti-Semitism. To be accepted in the rebellion, Jews must perform an extirpation of self, the same rite of death and transfiguration by which the anti-Semite Richard Wagner conceded that Jews might save their souls. For, the real, unregenerate Jews, the Jews as a body, are, like all whites but in their own special, tradition-haunted way, racists, practicers of cultural genocide, odious aggressors intent on neocolonial oppression of the colored brothers in the Middle East. They are so inherently different from all that is black and beautiful that only an act of supreme self-renunciation will permit a Jew-boy to save his potential soul.

This situation, submitted to (perhaps with suppressed pain) by some Jewish radicals, is exceedingly hard for Jewish liberals and left liberals to bear. Liberals are at a disadvantage in general in the current argument. Not only are they out-maneuvered when assigned to the odious position of an establishment whose values are questioned. *Their* voices are not customarily raised with the stridency required today. If they can make themselves heard at all over the heckling, it is only to apologize and explain.

Even considering these difficulties it is remarkable how little attention liberals, and especially liberal Jews, pay to the very outspoken expressions of those who now attack them. When it is a question of their own responses, they show the highest sensitivity to anything in matter or tone that might possibly offend. But they demonstrate an extraordinary insensitivity to assaults upon themselves, if attack comes from the right quarter. Not only are they resolutely immune to insult; they are triply armor-plated and impenetrable to offensive ideas among those who, in their view, should be in their camp. They simply ignore *what* is being said, in their anxiety not to notice *how* it is being said, and assume that nothing has changed essentially in the values of the world as they once knew it.

In spite of their deference to black militancy, liberal Jews cannot submit without pain and shock (and, when the controls slip, outright resentment) to being simply lumped with "whitey." Nor do they really care, even by association with the blacks, to have their dissociation from other Americans too sharply underlined either. They still like to believe that Jews and Negroes share with other Americans supreme values, against which the existing differences are trivial. But if attention must regrettably be drawn to areas in which Jews and Negroes differ from other

15

Americans, liberal Jews wish to assume that what Jews and
Negroes have in common, even in this joint difference, is the
paramount feature of their relationship.

In a symposium on "Negro and Jew: An Encounter in America," organized in 1966 by *Midstream* magazine, these were
some of the questions participants were asked to respond to:

"Do Jews, because of the ethics of their religion, and because
of their historical experience as a persecuted group, owe a
special debt of greater participation in the Negro liberation
movement than their Christian neighbors? . . . Have the rab-
binate, . . . and the lay Jewish organizations, contributed their
proper share to the Negro liberation movement? . . . Has the
Negro leadership done its full duty to counteract anti-Jewish
sentiments among the Negro masses?"

Midstream, a Zionist-sponsored journal, is far less given to the
clichés of Jewish liberalism (a term, by the way, that deserves
specific discussion) than other Jewish literary-political maga-
zines. But even here the initial assumption is that Jews and
Negroes belong together. This is the nearly universal assumption
among Jewish writers, and among many of the older Negro
intellectuals and leaders.

It shows in the special, indignant note of surprise and resentment that always creeps into "dialogues" on contemporary
Negro-Jewish relations; perhaps more surprise than resentment
on the Jewish side and more resentment than surprise on the
Negro side, but always resentment. Discussion *begins* with
formulas of mutual recrimination: have the Jews, "because of
their historical experience as a persecuted group, a special debt,"
and have they "contributed their proper share"; or has the
Negro leadership "done its full duty"? The quarrel becomes
especially painful because it is assumed to be a family quarrel.

The question is whether making this assumption is a healthy
way to approach the issues. The question is whether we do not
blind ourselves, by seeing only the ways in which Jews and

16

Negroes belong together, to the equally, if not more, important fact that there are many significant ways in which they do not belong together at all; and may indeed have conflicting interests.

Such self-induced blindness should have lost all credibility anyway ever since the slogan of "black power" gave a name to facts that grew increasingly obvious over the years. The name "black power" is, no doubt, a vague one, and is likely to remain so as long as Negro leaders believe that to define it specifically would cause too much damage to their movement through ideological disputes and divisions. But its fundamental emotional meaning is quite clear. (And for knowledgeable Jews, it is worth noting that it means exactly the same as the equally vague term of "autoemancipation" with which Jewish nationalism began in the 1880's.) The blacks wanted to run their own show in the mid-1960's, without always worrying about the susceptibilities of whites: even—or especially—of white liberals and even—or especially—those with powerful positions in the civil rights movement. They wanted to be militant in their own style: nonviolent only if it got them the results *they* desired, not merely the approbation of white pacifists; politically involved, mainly for *their own,* specific, black community ends, not the common interest in building a progressive society.

It is an unpleasant and revealing fact that when the slogan of "black power" was first adopted, it hit white liberals, and especially Jewish liberals, in a way that riots in Harlem and Watts never did. When Negroes burned down the slums they lived in, their rejection of the *whole* of white society was grim and brutal enough to make anyone with an open mind understand. But white liberals were so incredibly smug that they thought they were not included; and those among them who indulged in their own modish forms of protest might even dare to identify with the destruction. When Jewish stores were singled out for burning and looting, in a new version of pogrom,

17

Jewish liberals did not feel involved. What did throw a scare into them was the announcement that Negroes intended to run their own "revolution." Here they felt menaced where it hurt them most, in their identity.

I am unable to sympathize with Jewish liberals who were shut out by the slogan of "black power," whereas I fully understood the Negroes who adopted the slogan. It was a curious piece of presumption to expect Negroes to maintain a "revolutionary" movement in such terms that whites could find fulfillment in it. Last of all could one weep for Jews who, finding themselves unable to live in complete, individual, alienated detachment after abandoning the community they were born in, hoped to lean on the Negro revolution and use this as the concrete foundation for an abstract, fictive community of protest. The solidarity and self-discipline of the Negro community is a serious matter. It is the beginning of self-respect and responsibility for them, and the essential prerequisite for anything else that may be done to advance their cause and welfare.

What is true of blacks is also true, in this case, of Jews. They, too, could gain from a secure sense of belonging with and responsibility for other Jews. For one thing, self-respect may well provide a basis for rational understanding with others on issues that are confused by self-rejection.

CRISIS MANAGEMENT

Shortly after the black revolution broke into the campus at San Francisco State University, Brandeis was one of the universities chosen for action on this new front. Black students occupied a building, containing the university's computer and central switchboard. In one way, this was part of a synchronized series of militant seizures directed in various parts of the country in 1968/69 against colleges and universities—that is, against the strongholds of white liberalism in America. At Brandeis, it

18

also represented a new phase in the rapidly evolving clash between black militants and American Jews.

Throughout the critical period, the Jewish aspect of the dispute was sedulously ignored by the faculty, student body, and administration. The black commandos, whose sense of propriety allowed them to proclaim the existence of Malcolm X University at Brandeis (thus openly enshrining an apostle of black anti-Semitism in a school not merely Jewish-sponsored but largely Jewish-populated), judged the situation correctly. No one took offense. For their part, the militants sugar-coated the Negro-Jewish aspect of the confrontation by using as one of their major spokesmen a Jewish black, a young man born of a Jewish mother, identified with Judaism by choice, trained at the local Hebrew Teachers College, and said to be planning a rabbinical career.

The conflict, as publicly defined by the parties, was between the educational demands of black nationalism and the established standards of a nonsectarian American university. On the side of the entrenched forces of Malcolm X University, a complicated, incoherent torrent of charges, demands, complaints, and accusations issued forth. These statements varied from time to time in response to tactical requirements, or to the balance of power in the black militant contingent and the changing delegations selected to deal with the university authorities. All the formulas and proclamations, however, pretended to be merely "clarification" of ten initially proclaimed demands, which were "non-negotiable."

On the side of the administration and faculty, positions were also fluctuating and rather obscure, but only on a few matters of basic academic principle were they placed initially beyond the scope of bargaining. The fundamental principle which, according to the faculty consensus, could not be compromised was the ultimate, sole authority of the academic staff to appoint its own members and determine the standards for admitting students,

19

teaching them, and qualifying them for graduation. These were said to be aspects of academic freedom basic to the very existence of a university in the American tradition. Everything else was negotiable; but not, of course, under the gun of a black occupation of university premises.

It was a curious scene, as it unfolded. The black students were, to all appearances, rigid on the method of bargaining—stating non-negotiable demands—but quite vague on matters of substance. The faculty as a party to the dispute seemed to take a firm stand on substantial issues and presented a highly flexible self-image on procedures. But in fact the reverse was true in both cases. The Afro-American rebels gave up, in effect, on the matter of procedures while the faculty, through the administration, surrendered in effect on issues of substance—with both sides attempting to save face by transparent pretenses.

The administration's tactics on this occasion have been generally admired as a brilliant demonstration of pragmatic white-liberal flexibility. Determined not to act provocatively or be provoked, Morris B. Abram, the new president of Brandeis, resisted all pressures to call in the police, and, instead, simply conducted the business of the university through emergency facilities. The occupied university nerve center was surgically bypassed and the blacks, self-isolated, were left to their own devices. After ten days, with midyear examinations about to begin and the administration still refusing to abandon the position defined by the faculty, the black students simply left the building—without concluding any negotiated settlement of the issues. But in the meantime the administration had arranged an informal poll indicating willingness of a probable majority of the faculty to accept one of the blacks' main substantive demands, the creation of a department of African and Afro-American studies; and following the evacuation of the occupied building, such a department was approved by formal faculty vote.

20

What, however, was the substantive issue involved in introducing a department of black studies at Brandeis? This was a question on which the faculty remained remarkably dumb. But anyone with the least sensitivity to the unspoken knew well enough what was involved. In terms of academic criteria, the discussion raised no more than technical, moot questions: Was there enough academic substance to the curriculum proposed for a black studies department? Were such "area studies," in general, appropriately conducted in the form of departments, or should departmental status be reserved for "disciplines"? But behind such debatable technicalities was another issue which for many, perhaps a majority, was neither technical nor really debatable. Should any kind of ethnic distinction among Americans be recognized at all in the Brandeis curriculum? The demand for a black studies department at Brandeis ran into the block raised for a considerable part of the faculty by their severe qualms over anything that hinted at another ethnic distinction of the university: that it was largely Jewish and, against serious inhibitions, recognized Jewish studies as a valid discipline.

What principle is involved here? It is hardly a real academic principle. The entire field of humanistic studies in every university is strongly divided into ethnic areas: history is chiefly taught as a collection of national histories, literature as a selection of national literatures. But Jews (and Negroes) in America are minorities: that is, they belong to a category whose distinctiveness had best be forgotten or, at least, reduced to tolerable dimensions.

The principle here no doubt faintly recalls an essential rule of the academic life—to ignore in the pursuit of knowledge whatever is merely subjective—and Jews who wish to hide from themselves in the academy often seek to cover themselves with this cloak. But the fear of black studies in a Jewish university springs far less from resistance to subjectivity in an academic discipline than from another source. It springs from the fear that the academic narcosis may be lifted from one's own Jewish subjectivity.

The issue, in any case, was handled with the deliberate fuzzy-mindedness, passing for flexibility, by which liberals protect themselves from the abhorred prospect of a confrontation. What the Brandeis Afro-Americans really wanted was apparent to anyone who allowed himself to listen. Their goal, moderately stated, was a regular academic department fully autonomous and fully recognized, where those black students (exclusively, or with a fringe of sympathetic whites) whom they would select would cultivate a black identity under black nationalist teachers chosen by a black nationalist director. The extremist version of this demand is simply to set up an indoctrination center and training academy for black militant activists. The role of Brandeis in all this would be simply to finance the project and confer the prestige of an academic degree from a well-regarded private university upon the graduates.

Nothing bedeviled the Brandeis negotiations of 1968/69 more than the white liberal academy's unwillingness to face, or inability to admit to itself, the true nature of the black demands. The hang-up from the beginning was a dreadful reluctance to say "no" to the black students. The real nationalist program of a department of black indoctrination *for* the black people, *of* the black people, and *by* the black people, could only be perceived by Jewish-liberal academics as a "specific program for racial segregation and discrimination"—as some bolder spirits, indeed, described it. In order to maintain the attitude of friendly reasonableness which, as the sociologists say, is "functionally imperative" for the high calling of education, the academics had to take these demands as mere emotional rhetoric, natural under the trying conditions of a black minority among whites. They had to tell themselves their students were fundamentally reasonable and, accordingly, what they really wanted must be something implied rather than stated: a tacit set of reasonable demands

22

—or, rather, what to an academic, too, could appear to be reasonable demands.

The result was that, for months before the crisis, faculty action on the nationalist program was based on faculty restatements of the essence of the demands in forms they found academically acceptable. Instead of a "department," the faculty committee on the matter proposed and gained approval for a "concentration": an arrangement for a degree based on a combination of studies, in various existing departments, which were "relevant" to black interests and also ensured more or less adequate training in standard academic disciplines. This meant, of course, no autonomy for blacks in shaping curriculum, hiring staff, and disposing of a separate budget. The seizure of the Brandeis communications center made it brutally clear that this was no solution.

The final consequence of the faculty's attempt to be reasonable and placatory was that the dispute settled down to a deadlock on the one point where the academy could not openly yield: the demand of the black nationalist society for a formally recognized, decisive voice in essentially academic questions, such as the appointment of a department head. The blacks, of course, did end their sit-in, and the faculty then did approve a "department"—with the significant qualification that it was to be a "legitimate" department: that is, one whose chairman and staff would be chosen in the normal way. This left all the critical academic questions still open: who formally and who in effect would appoint the chairman of the new department? Who formally and who in effect would determine which black students (not to say how many) would be admitted to Brandeis?

What, then, was the net result of the faculty's sincere and well-intentioned maneuvers? The first consequence was an explosion of catcalls and vituperation from the Brandeis Afro-American society: "Lies! Lies! Lies!" They charged that the president and faculty were deliberately seeking to manipulate

23

public opinion by pretending to deal with black demands, while in fact they dealt only with their own dishonest interpretations of such demands. By mutual consent—or by mutual reluctance to push confrontation to conclusions—the crisis was ended without agreement. It left a situation of repressed conflict and an institution shaken but still intact. The possibilities were these: if the black students ultimately accomplished their declared purpose, they would organize a recognized school of black nationalist indoctrination, agitation, and other political action at Brandeis, and the academy would have abdicated its function; if the faculty accomplished its declared purpose, the black students could be condemned for having sold out to Whitey; and if neither principle won a clear victory, then muddy compromise formulas, resolving the situation by evading the issue, would continuously generate ill will and prepare the ground for future conflict. The last is what in fact occurred in the period after the crisis.

Underlying the black-liberal conflict at Brandeis there was also an unmentioned Negro-Jewish communal conflict. What might have happened if *this* issue had been openly faced and dealt with directly from the beginning? Much of the confusion and backbiting need never have happened if it were possible —which, for reasons too obvious to mention, it was not—for some members of the Brandeis faculty to approach the black demands first as Jews before they resumed their academic hats.

The notion that black studies are vital to those seeking to build a black identity; the idea that, if instituted in a university, such studies should be conducted in a spirit the black community accepts: these notions could hardly shock and repel Jews secure in their own identity as they do the detached academic. Any Jew negotiating this demand would deal with it at once, directly, in its own terms.

His first item of negotiation would certainly have been a matter that no one at Brandeis during the crisis cared to mention openly. He would insist that the personnel and curriculum of a black studies department at Brandeis could under no circumstances be anti-Semitic. Much was said at the time about elements of the black demands incompatible with the university's existence; but this publicly ignored item was a matter which—if one were foolish enough to disregard it in fact—could certainly, in a very concrete sense, destroy Brandeis. Black nationalists might then indignantly deny that they were anti-Semites, which would have been a very healthy development. But it is hard to imagine them dealing with this matter as they did with the academics' proposed substitution of a "concentration" for the "department" demanded by the blacks. No one, least of all the black nationalists, could expect to carry much conviction by claiming that when Jews seek to protect themselves against anti-Semites it is a subterfuge and a phony tactic.

An agreement between Jews and blacks on the validity and the character of a black studies department was entirely possible, without repressed misunderstandings on either side. Once achieved, it would open the way for a fully worked-out program designed to meet technical academic requirements. For this is the level to which questions that still at bottom divide the parties at Brandeis would be reduced by an ethnic approach. Once the outlines and details of a black studies department had been worked out to the satisfaction of Negroes and Jews, the question of formulating the agreement in terms consonant with existing academic procedures would never have become an issue dividing them. It would be a joint problem, the same for both.

Both sides would take the rules essential to an academic community as a condition of life imposed by the larger framework which belongs to neither alone, excluding the other, but includes both alike. In this way the essential principles of the academy would have been formally acknowledged by Jews and Negroes alike, after the underlying ethnic issues, essentially

25

immaterial to the academy, had been directly confronted and settled by the parties.

The actual outcome was in some ways the same, but in some ways significantly different. Issues were resolved, to the extent they were settled, on the basis of underlying ethnic concerns. They were argued, to the extent they were publicly dealt with, in academic terms. What was actually established thus approximated, more or less, what might have resulted from direct ethnic negotiations. But instead of direct, open, conclusive, rational agreements there were indirect, more or less disguised, irritatingly extended dealings ending in arrangements neither entirely rational nor entirely honest. As for the principles essential to the academy, they were evaded instead of being formally acknowledged and effectively applied.

CRISIS MISMANAGEMENT

During the Brandeis crisis, another Negro-Jewish confrontation was taking place in the Ocean Hill-Brownsville section of New York. If Brandeis suffered from dealing with essentially ethnic questions as though they were academic, Ocean Hill-Brownsville suffered because certain essentially trade union issues were dealt with as though they were ethnic. And here too a more rational and generally satisfactory solution of the real ethnic problems involved could well have been achieved, or at least approached, if these matters, instead of basically unrelated questions, had been directly considered in ethnic terms.

In Ocean Hill-Brownsville, as at Brandeis, Negroes clashed with Jews over educational and professional issues. Again, the Jewish side was not constituted nor did it conduct itself, like the local Negro community, on the principle of representing explicit ethnic interests. The blacks demanded local community control of the schools, including in particular authority to hire or fire personnel at their discretion: an open black nationalist

26

position. The other side stood in defense of trade union and civil service principles. They fought for the sanctity, security, and binding validity in local districts of their centrally negotiated contracts and they upheld established rights of tenure and of due process for the protection of teachers against arbitrary transfer or dismissal.

But other circumstances, which produced in Ocean Hill-Brownsville and throughout New York City an atmosphere of violence avoided at Brandeis, also brought into the open the underlying ethnic conflict. Militants on the fringe of the black camp of embattled parents and community leaders whipped up fury with blatant anti-Semitic slogans and propaganda. The teachers' union, giving wide publicity to these black extremist activities, rallied city-wide Jewish support for their cause. Instead of being repressed, the underlying ethnic conflict was actively agitated and, some say, inflated.

These were inevitable consequences in New York, however smoothly they were elided and avoided in Waltham. At Brandeis, the initial use of force came from a small group of black students among an overwhelmingly white, Jewish, and peaceably well-disposed academic community. Once the wise decision not to react with force was taken, the potential for violence was successfully contained. At Brandeis, too, black militancy immediately threatened no major material interest of the whites. In Ocean Hill-Brownsville, however, the aggressive initiative and force came from a militant leadership solidly based in the local black community. It threatened a small group of white teachers with serious material harm, and involved vital professional interests of teachers throughout the city. Under such circumstances, the masterful restraint of the Brandeis administration, exercised from a position of dominant power and relative safety, would have been totally irrelevant and, of course, impossible. It is hard to see how any policy other than militant resistance could have been applied by a professional group to the

27

kind of attack launched by the Ocean Hill community. That the teachers, mainly Jewish, should also see it as a Jewish issue was not only an advantage to their cause, but a reflection of the reality of the situation.

Serious threats to the interests of established groups must necessarily occur in the course of the black revolution. On numerous occasions before and since Ocean Hill-Brownsville black demands have produced conflicts openly defined as ethnic. Polish neighborhoods, Italian construction workers, Irish school committees, and similar concentrations of ethnic power have been challenged by Negro militants in an atmosphere of undisguised ethnic hostility on both sides. But in none of these cases could the clash produce the very specific, far-reaching, and highly complex involvement that is inevitable whenever Jews are concerned and anti-Semitism is invoked.

It is not simply that Jew-hatred calls up an age-old prejudice universally present among Gentiles and absorbed at such a primal childhood level that adult sophistication can rarely dissipate it completely. It is not simply that hating Jews means automatically joining a majority, as perspicacious Negro critics like James Baldwin were the first to point out and as is now well understood even among politically alert black teenagers. Nor is it simply the fact that Jew-hatred often fails to meet the prompt, instinctive backlash that occurs when Poles, Italians, or Irishmen are attacked. In the face of the perennial, nearly universal hostility they have encountered, many Jews, like old-time Negroes, developed a protective habit of deafness, dumbness, and blindness, frequently preferring to pretend the viciousness was not there rather than provoke it to greater fury by openly opposing it.

Anti-Semitism, sharply distinguished in all these respects from any ordinary ethnic hostility, has still another, currently important distinction. Other ethnic clashes are essentially confined to the area and issues directly involved. Whenever Jews are concerned there is the constant possibility that the loosely connected international fellowship of political anti-Semites will come into the picture. No well-publicized incident of Jew-hatred can long escape the attention of that curious collection of fanatics and professional agitators. They are linked by bizarre connections which put former Nazi propagandists at the service of Egyptian anti-Israeli agencies, feed materials (and according to some, more direct support) financed by Arab oil revenues into the organs of black nationalist activism, and join Left radicals or Maoists with epigones of WASP fascist anti-Semitism in a common anti-Israeli and anti-Jewish front. A hatred which links Hitler with Stalin, George Lincoln Rockwell with Malcolm X, Haj Amin el Husseini (erstwhile Mufti of Jerusalem and main Muslim Nazi agent during World War II) with the Olympian Arnold Toynbee, Ezra Pound with Josef Goebbels; a hatred which not only gives men like these—in many cases, blood-foes—a common basis of understanding but allows them to consider and sometimes carry out joint political activities: such a hatred is no ordinary ethnic hostility.

The overtones of such political anti-Semitism rang out clearly amid the varied clamor of black agitation in Ocean Hill-Brownsville. This made the hush-hush approach tacitly adopted at Brandeis impossible. The anti-Semitic expressions noted could not be accepted at the level of bad manners and reaction confined to what was proper at that level. These expressions were decoded by the Jewish community's perception as announcing a threat of the kind whose vicious potentialities were all too familiar. Nothing but a violent rejoinder, a stiff posture of self-defense, was an adequate response to such a challenge for Jews of this generation.

The Jewish response which came was therefore well justified and, to a significant degree, effective. Angry Negro disclaimers were issued—and echoed by some Jewish liberals and Jewish institutions—denying that anti-Semitism was an important element in the Ocean Hill situation. The teachers' union was charged with inflating the issue deliberately for its own ends, and there was bitter complaint that no effort was made to understand the deeper sources of Negro hostility. One might agree, within limits, with the latter contentions without accepting the former. Only the Jews' indignation at anti-Semitic expressions and actions—undeniably present, however important or unimportant in the total picture of Ocean Hill—produced the disclaimers of anti-Semitism that followed. From a Jewish ethnic point of view *political* anti-Semitism is important whenever it appears, and we can never, by our silent acquiescence, grant it any appearance of legitimacy.

But does this mean there was a clear Jewish ethnic interest at stake in the teachers' union's demands? This is certainly a far more difficult and complex problem than any involved, for example, in the situation at Brandeis. Nathan Glazer is one serious observer of the ethnic scene who argues that careers open to talent and, in consequence, uneven concentration of ethnic groups by occupations and social positions according to demonstrated merit in equal competition are not only high American principles but vital American-Jewish interests. The interest of American Negroes, however, demands the abandonment of those principles and the allocation of social positions and rewards on a quota plan. From this standpoint, the hostility of Ocean Hill to Jewish teachers and their civil service principles expressed a real and clear ethnic conflict.

But in spite of the fact that so many teachers involved were Jews, it is not at all clear that, in the long view, they represented unequivocal ethnic interests. Safeguards against excessively local control and maintaining established personnel procedures, even in experimental school districts, were of crucial importance to the union. They were not necessarily so to the Jews, as an ethnic duty. The ethnic duty is to see that Jews who are teachers are not abused or harmed materially in the course of advancing Negro demands. But Jewish interest does not necessarily require continued heavy concentration of Jews in any given profession or any particular non-Jewish locality. An ethnic strategy might well suggest that it is a Jewish interest, whatever the Negro interest may be, to help phase out endangered Jews from hostile black school districts, as is being done with Jewish storekeepers.

This is not to suggest that there are any simple answers. Marshall Sklare, for one, decries the ease with which we contemplate the uprooting of Jewish lower-middle-class communities, the aging storekeepers, in the face of the threatening black ghetto. It may be highly American to be so mobile, he points out, but there might be greater ethnic wisdom in standing ground and defending the turf, as Poles, Italians, and Irishmen do. And even if one considers it the best policy—whether on grounds of a mobile Americanism, human equities, or ethnic principles—to move over and make room for the blacks, there is obviously a great difference between relocating a declining group of aging storekeepers and moving out a large group of active professionals, constituting a major part of a school system. Not all of them believe they can do better for themselves, ethnically if not materially, by moving to Israel. Nor can they be easily replaced in Brooklyn.

What is clear, in any case, is that nothing is gained by doctrinaire attitudes, however idealistic; and that where ethnic interests are at stake, nothing is gained by ignoring them or cloaking them in irrelevant "principles." If the dispute in Ocean Hill-Brownsville had been handled, not only by Negroes but also by Jews, in terms of ethnic interests and by an organized ethnic community, it might possibly have taken a more civilized and rational course from the outset.

RELATIONS BETWEEN COMMUNITIES

"Would it prove helpful," asked the editor of *Midstream* of participants in his symposium on the Negro-Jewish encounter in America, "to establish special Negro-Jewish consultative bodies to examine misunderstandings between the two groups as these arise, and to foster greater understanding between them on the basis of common historical experiences of oppression, dispersion and minority status? . . . Do Jews (because of this common background) owe a special debt of greater participation in the Negro liberation movement?"

Conditions change with times, and the same blacks who once expelled white liberals and radicals from their liberation movement may one day want them back in. But there are basic reasons why any ethnic group, particularly under such pressures as prevail in America, should wish to keep outsiders at a distance. At a time of keen rivalry for the leading position in the community, white contributions to Negro organizations are not necessarily helpful. Why should white support, given in greater measure to one rather than another black liberation or civil rights organization, be an important factor in deciding which group wins out in the competition? Jews do not exactly welcome it when Jewish organizations, by publicity or solicitation or channels of influence among Gentiles, claim a larger place in Jewish affairs than we ourselves are ready to grant them. If "black power" means the right to keep whites on the sidelines while the community is organizing and deciding its future, it is a healthy and laudable principle.

"Black power" may also mean (no matter what those who invented the phrase intended) a general sanction for every impulse to reckless, purposeless violence in the Negro community. Gangs of juvenile delinquents who shout political slogans continue to act, nevertheless, as juvenile delinquents. Anti-Semites, who are elevated to the rank of black nationalists, remain anti-Semites. When Jews are asked to understand them, it makes no more sense than it did when we were asked to see in a proper revolutionary light the regrettable violence committed by Ukrainian peasants or Russian and Polish workers during pogroms. We can understand them easily enough—for the history of

Zionism knows its own violent excesses—but it is not our business to understand them. As Jews it is our business to resist pogroms, protest against them, and demand that responsible leaders and authorities control them.

The basis for any healthy Negro-Jewish relation, when the area of "black power" is touched, is to realize that we are not dealing with a family quarrel, but with the distinct and maybe even conflicting interests of separate groups. It was not only puerile and self-indulgent of Jews to protest against their exclusion from Negro affairs because of the "black power" slogan; it would have been foolish and self-destructive of the Negroes to take any other course. So, too, it is a pointless evasion for Negroes to try to explain the roots of black anti-Semitism to Jews. This problem child is not our child, no matter how liberal we may be, and it is not our business to understand him, but to insist he behaves. Only the illusion that we are all one big family, sharing precisely the same responsibilities, still confuses this issue, to the detriment of all concerned.

This cuts two ways, of course. It is pretty useless for Jews to scold Negro leaders for black anti-Semitism, as if they were our naughty siblings. On a moral plane, we *are* all brothers, but if Negro leaders needed only preaching to in order to control anti-Semitism they would have done the job long ago. The task involves a tricky problem in intracommunity politics, just as the job of controlling Zionist terrorist organizations did in its time. It is, in the same way, a task the Negro leadership will someday have to accomplish in its own interest, if it does not wish to lose control to irresponsible elements, and with it, the hope of a brighter Negro future. Our moralizing is of little effect here.

It follows that no great reliance can be placed in Negro-Jewish consultative bodies, if their aim is merely "to foster greater understanding . . . on the basis of common historical experiences of oppression, dispersion and minority status." If

33

there were such bodies devoted to examining conflicts of interest, and not mere misunderstandings, as they arise between the two groups, it would be another, far more serious matter. Just how serious such an effort would be, what important consequences it might entail, how grave the problems it might confront, and how slight the prospect of a full and successful attack can barely be imagined.

The basic Negro-Jewish conflict is the same as the basic black-white conflict, in specific application. What the Negro wants is whatever the white has, and he wants it *now*. The whites who have what Negroes are going to want to take *next* are very often Jews. The stores in Harlem, the teaching jobs and civil service appointments are rungs on the ladder that Negroes have to climb over the toes of Jews, just as they have to crowd Irishmen and Italians in the construction trades. These are the issues likely to concern any Jewish-Negro consultative committee that might usefully arise.

When such issues are raised by way of teenage gangs on the rampage with bricks and torches, we can treat them in no other way than as a kind of pogrom. If they are brought up as a matter of social equity for joint deliberation, we have to meet them on their merits. By this I do not mean a pious mouthing of liberal phrases about freedom and opportunity. That kind of talk belongs in brotherhood meetings where we assume we are all one big family. Here we have to deal with interests of groups—conflicting interests, indeed—which can only be satisfied by direct action. Merely to adopt such an agenda means that one undertakes not to illustrate a principle (of formally equal opportunity and reward according to merit) but to achieve a result (the equalization of Negro social and economic status); although it should be clear that this result can never be secure and permanent unless and until Negroes are able to sustain equality under conditions of equal opportunity, not preference, and reward according to merit, not need. For this goal to be achieved *next,* and as nearly as possible *now,* Negroes would have to demand that Jews, among others, make room for them; and Jews would have to consider how this could be done at the least possible cost to Jews. Whatever the ultimate benefits, to Jews as well as Negroes, it could certainly never be done without cost.

The dimensions of the problem are great; and the obstacles to solution are quite as great. For what is implied is, on both the Negro and the Jewish side, a disciplined, functional community organization. The Negroes can make demands, of course, without such an organization; but they can do very little without it to take advantage of whatever responses they may elicit. The Jews could neither carry out any program to make room for Negroes at the immediate expense of Jews, nor could they help find suitable new adjustments for Jews who might be affected, with the loose kind of quasi-organization the community now possesses.

The possibilities of an ethnic approach, in either case, are limited by a major, overriding consideration. American Jews and Negroes can never face each other as fully self-determining, separate entities, for they are both part of a larger American community. Any issue between them is necessarily complicated by the demands of the larger framework. In these circumstances an approach to ethnic disputes in ethnic terms can often eliminate irrelevancies, but it can never simplify issues to the point of escaping the broader involvement. Also, the demands of the common American framework limit the extent to which ethnic communal organization can be effectively achieved. But an optimum may well be sought—and in the opposite direction from current trends among the Jews and among the Negroes.

No reasonable ethnic policy can conceivably be followed by Negroes on the basis of opting out of the American community. Whatever the abstract ethical justification for a policy of black secession, to pursue it would neither unite the Negroes nor

35

produce a viable relationship with whites in this country. This is an issue which must be fought out in the Negro community before a truly reasonable basis for solving the critical problems of black Americans can begin to be built.

About the Jewish community one must say precisely the opposite. It has been a fatal delusion of American Jewry that in order to be American it has to be effectively disorganized. As long as Jews function as an ethnic body only by impulsive response and in the face of imminent dangers, they cannot deal with their future reasonably. A community so crippled not only harms itself but unnecessarily complicates its relations with everyone who comes in significant contact with it.

*　　　*　　　*

These reflections are provoked, of course, by the immediate situation and events of the recent past. But the Jews and blacks in America have long been perceived as stubborn and, perhaps, permanent problems, resisting analysis and solution by the methods that seemed to be working for other Americans. The present difficulties which they present to America-at-large and to each other stem from the basic exceptionalism of the Jewish and Negro situations. This essay is an attempt, if not to solve, then at least to understand the complex, perennial, fundamental problems of the two classic American minorities.

II.   The Classic Minorities

WE are living in a turbulent time and everything is notoriously open to change. If not the things themselves, at least the names we call them are being freely and radically altered. In the arbitrary usage of the moment, "minorities" means Negroes, Puerto Ricans, and certain other designated "third world" peoples exclusively. Any Jew who is not hiding from himself knows that this use of the term "minority"—which of course, has always been a loaded word, subject to abuse—ignores the reality he directly experiences by excluding him.

Some radical Jews, notably Arthur Waskow and his Washington group, the Jews for Urban Justice, say that Jews themselves are to blame for not being accredited as a minority. They have been false to their identity and worshipped the Golden Calf. They have bowed down to the monolith of a repressive, authoritarian America, instead of joining with other minorities, like true Jews, to "crack" the monolith in order to recompose from its fragments a liberated, pan-minority America. For what America most needs is to destroy the false majority status of its varied combinations of privileged minorities.

What all this means is far from clear; except that it has a pointed affinity with radically separatist black nationalism—a rather cool and disdainful ally with whom such schools of Jewish activists yearn to be united. But it is more than doubtful that a really radical pluralism, consistent down to its ultimate consequences, is possible for America or desired by the followers and fellow-travelers of these pseudo-Messianists, whether Jewish or black. Pan-minority America without a majority is, at best, a utopia. Moreover, the idea misrepresents the wishes and felt needs of the minority masses, who, as Americans, do require a majority to integrate them.

Yet, terms and ideas the older generation once played with were not a more accurate guide to the actual situation or to what Americans really desired. Old-line America was always reluctant to admit that it had ethnic or religious or any other kind of minorities. The classic American tradition held that our nationhood, like Renan's French conception of the nation, was based on a *plébiscite de tous les jours;* it derived directly from the individual citizen's pledge of allegiance to our democratic political principles. Hence, religion was irrelevant to it, race was irrelevant to it, and even culture, other than the specifically civic culture of the Republic, was theoretically irrelevant to it. On this assumption, we had no majority in belief, descent, or Old World traditions that was entitled to demand conformity to its values; and accordingly there could be, in principle, no religious, racial, or ethnic minorities.

Not only the general public but American social scientists, who pride themselves on fact-finding and objectivity, preferred to avoid the suggestion of unequal rights in the word "minority." They used instead such terms as "subculture." A word prefaced by "sub" may suggest a degree of conflict, in the implied *subordination* of the minority culture and community to the majority; but the main connotation is that of the *harmonious inclusion* of the subculture and subcommunity in the more comprehensive culture and community of the nation as a whole. For "subculture" or "subcommunity" imply something that is not real and complete in itself but it requires a whole culture and community in order to exist.

No one thought it necessary to invent a parallel term for the majority—such as "superculture," perhaps. The identity between Old (or, as we now say, WASP) Americans and the *real* America was so complete that no sociological tag was needed to describe the relationship. But silence on this point could also suggest that no majority existed.

In fact, of course, there was always a dominant group that felt entitled to demand conformity to its values. While vaguely defined and variable in composition from issue to issue, there was a consensus of opinion that determined what kind of religion was approved, and to what extent; which racial types were admitted to which positions; and which ethnic cultures were proper for what occasions. Old-line America might in this way eventually absorb, after proper processing, groups of not-yet-real-Americans who awaited full assimilation. But in the meantime, and in fact, America had religious, racial, ethnic majorities and minorities.

In those not so old but nearly forgotten days, a simple conception of the way newcomers could be "Americanized" was generally accepted. The public view was that the old settlers, the real Americans, had established an open society based on the American Way of Life: on freedom of belief and opinion and free enterprise. Participation in it was open, in principle, to anyone according to his individual merit. There was no discrimination—but admission to the real America was subject to a test of individual performance.

Also, while anyone could seek admission, no one was compelled to apply simply because he lived here. Citizenship alone was not the sole and final gateway to the real America, in spite of our theory that Americanism was essentially a political allegiance. The liberal principles of an open society applied theoretically throughout the society. Hence, the real American was one whose performance as a liberalist was successfully tested in all social spheres, not only in the functions of the state. Such tests are by nature optional. So one could continue even as a citizen, let alone as a resident alien, to refuse tests of Americanism, and to seclude oneself voluntarily from the open society in whatever enclave of tolerated segregation one chose.

39

This arrangement was favored, among other reasons, by the largeness and looseness of America, a continental nation. The sheer amplitude of America allowed it to live with a considerable shapelessness of over-all structure. Subcultures and subcommunities could be tolerated side by side with the real America. This left the ultimate form of their mutual relation to be determined: in theory, by a free interchange of ideas and influences in which newcomers had equal access to the market with the settled Americans; but in practice by applying liberalistic principles already built into the structure of the Old American society which the newcomers, presumably, still had to learn.

Free entry into American society had its price, and also its restrictions. In theory, the ultimate form of the mutual relationship between Old and New America might be an open issue, susceptible to influence even from the newcomers. But the condition was implied of the willingness of the immigrant to give up old, inherited forms. America was the New World, come to redress the balance of the Old, to replace it by something bigger and better. Everyone in it, in principle, had turned his back on the corrupt Old World; and, in order to enter, newcomers had to be willing to do the same. This was *the price* of assimilation into the real America, the preliminary test and condition that must be met.

The *limits* of assimilation were defined by the established prerogatives of the older settlers. It was implicitly, or explicitly, assumed that those who came here first were entitled to preserve, and others were obliged to respect, what they had built into the American Way of Life. This naturally included the old settlers' social status as well as their traditional values.

The American idea of proper social organization was not that of a totally unstratified, unsegregated, undifferentiated society, but of a society with class differences and loose, permeable segregations, open to the passage of individuals who proved their worth. Assimilation was regarded as a process of testing

40

the achievements of newcomers in acquiring whatever was necessary to being a good American; and, to make the test effective, the barriers behind which the real Old Americans were entrenched had to be maintained at appropriate graded heights— each in turn not too high, yet not too low. Ideally only a man's intrinsic merit should count in his rise to the inner circle, where his business or professional success would parallel his acceptance of, and acceptance into, the intimacies and values of the best American society.

Class lines were not maintained by fixing the proper station of each group, as, for example, in Europe. No formal or customary codes of exclusion grounded in law or religion constitutionally reserved special rights and privileges for particular families, estates, castes, or sects. The position of the older settlers was maintained by informal, almost tacit covenants, which only rarely (as in our Immigration Acts) needed to be openly expressed. Not the results were predetermined, but the rules and procedures were defined under which cultural change and social mobility could take place within the established pattern.

CULTURE AND CLASS IN OLD AMERICA

The theory was, as said, that the American Way was open to change; it encouraged the free expression of individuality. Hence the fact that certain established ways enjoyed a *de facto* constitutional status when immigrants arrived need not, in principle, prevent newcomers from influencing future development in their own individual ways. Once they had caught up with already achieved expressions of American freedom, they were at liberty, if they could, to lead American institutions in new directions. They might even naturalize characteristic values out of their own immigrant heritage. The only thing ruled out, in principle, was to try to lead America back to characteristically Old World institutions.

These phrases, of course, merely pose a problem. How was

41

one to decide, in practice, whether any immigrant custom, institution, or cultural offering was a legitimately American expression of individuality or must be condemned as an Old World relic? A tacitly understood rule of thumb served as a pragmatic test: if any group of newcomers was not ashamed to make a public display of its folkways or Old World loyalties, and particularly if other Americans became familiar with them and learned to appreciate them, they—or reasonable facsimiles adapted to American taste—became authentic features of the American scene. In this way, over the years, St. Patrick's Day, chop suey, pizzas, and kosher dill pickles have become almost as American as the Fourth of July. But anything that was better kept closed off and private, any collective intimacy shared only by one group of newcomers and not basically accessible to all others, was stamped as Old World clannishness. Such separatism was certainly permissible in the immigrant ghetto, but it signified an unwillingness to be "integrated" into the real America.

To carry out the cultural selection this suggests, there must be something in the nature of a "general social consensus" able to pass judgment on the Americanism of novelties submitted for general approval. In democratic America, all citizens might expect to be, and are in some sense, judges of each other's cultural and institutional offerings; and (as in an election) the rough balance of their appreciation or disdain decides the acceptance or rejection, or specific evaluation, of everything made public in the American panorama.

We are governed in all spheres of life, not only in politics, by a tyrannous majority, as we know since Tocqueville. But it is not a simple numerical majority. The equality of all our judges is an equality affected with a difference. In those days (it remains to be seen what changes our own radical times may have introduced) the Old Americans had an established position and sat in the box seats, rarely, if ever, on the platform, of the all-American cultural popularity contest.

Radical, freewheeling innovations were frequent among Old Americans themselves, in view of the loose and open character of the American tradition, both frontier and urban. One need only think of American revivalism and denominationalism, of Joseph Smith and Mary Baker Eddy, of writers like Poe, Melville, Whitman, Hawthorne, of Henry James or Henry Adams to appreciate the range and variability of the native culture. But when such homegrown products were accepted or rejected, the Old Americans alone (including those whom they adopted into the inner circle of "native sons," but not the immigrants and other probationary and neophyte Americans) determined the consensus. For, values institutionalized by *their* approval formed the privileged, nuclear core of the American Way of Life. These were the values that had a serious claim to the intellectual and emotional adherence of *all* Americans. The jury that approved them had to be a blue ribbon jury, made up of those who were fully, authentically American.

When immigrant novelties made a public debut, they rarely claimed such serious attention or presented themselves immediately to so august a jury. Outgroup cultures got their first encouragement to feel at home in America in the new territories and polyglot ghettos where Poles and French Canadians, Swedes and Germans, Slovaks and Hungarians, Irish, Italians, Jews (and later Negroes) met one another. They met "marginally" and, at first, only to clash. But soon, too, they began to appreciate and enjoy their differences; particularly those trivialities that were easiest to enjoy. Light, entertaining, superficial traits are what a group naturally chooses to display when self-mockery is the quickest way to become popular. Newcomers who expect mockery will keep private whatever is most intimate and taken most seriously.

What has pleased one s neighbors may then gain acceptance in America at large. In this way, jazz became as clearly a part of the American Way as Puritanism. Italian grand opera, Wagnerian music drama, and Irish politicians came to be taken seriously by a broad cross-section of Americans, not only by the immigrants who brought them over. But never, of course, as seriously as the Protestant ethic, Baptist or Methodist evangelism, or the attenuated high-mindedness of Boston Brahmins.

One could set up a status scale for various groups in America according to whether they usually present themselves to the public in a serious or comic vein. Old Americans felt so integrated with the American Way of Life that they identified their most intimate and serious preoccupations with our "native philosophy"; and other Americans were ready to acknowledge this claim. This was the accepted basis of our general social consensus. New immigrants might find acceptance for external, relatively trivial features of their tradition, but they marked themselves as different by their more serious and intimate collective expressions. These were fostered, if at all, outside the real America. They were private. Because they had to be kept private, groups collectively organized around a nucleus of such values occupied a lower status in the scale of American social class.

*   *   *

A truly liberal philosophy has difficulty in dealing with the kind of privacy that is shared by a group. The privacy of the individual is essential to liberalism; but if the whole of society —the economy and the class structure, as well as the state—is to be organized on the principle of freedom, private reserves of closed groups should not exist. They set up intolerable barriers to the free movement of men and talents upon which a liberalistic society essentially depends.

There are, nevertheless, two major opportunities for recognizing what we may call group privacy which have always been part of the social philosophy native to Old America. One such

44

possibility is summed up by the maxim that a man's business
—and by this we usually mean his home and family as well—is
his private affair. The other, signalized in this country by the
separation of church and state, is the principle that religion is a
private affair.

The acceptance as private and protected of whatever is a
man's own business—his residence, his neighborhood, his personal intimates, his kin, his property—is the foundation that
upholds the various social segregations that still characterize us,
in spite of American egalitarianism. Not only one's family but
one's friends and acquaintances, not only one's home but one's
club and neighborhood, not only the family firm but the cor-
poration were accepted in Old America as legitimate spheres of
freedom where a man might choose his intimates and associates
on grounds of personal preference.

If this led to exclusions which ran along lines of racial,
ethnic, or religious discrimination, it was, according to the most
common Old American view, a *de facto* consequence of freedom
quite natural and acceptable in our tradition. Others would
deny that what had happened was, in fact, a significant exclusion
or deliberate discrimination according to color, creed, or national origin. They conceded that there was a snobbish set who
were not satisfied with success in business but expected an Old
American lineage and eligibility for baptismal, nuptial, and
burial rites in one of the fashionable churches as conditions for
acceptance in the best American society. But, the true inner
circle that governed the real America was a more liberally recruited elite, open to all who proved themselves, without discrimination according to race, creed, or color. The closed social
circles, whether of Old Americans or of the immigrants themselves, did not really set our standards or determine our values.
They were minor, or major, eddies which did not divert the
mainstream of America from its course.

The privacy of religious belief was a somewhat different

matter. The segregations it set up were recognized *de jure,* not merely *de facto.* The class structure built on the privacy of one's own business is certainly a serious, not a trivial matter; but in theory at least, it permits and encourages the movement of individuals from class to class on the sole test of performance. The standards underlying it are, in theory, common to all Americans without discrimination, though of course more natural to old settlers than to the not yet acculturated new. The privacy of religion means recognizing an irreducible difference of values that, quite explicitly, legitimately, and, in principle, permanently segregates groups of Americans.

To say no more than this would be to describe inaccurately the true institutional position of religion in Old America. If religion is considered a private affair, all religions must be equally tolerated: Islam, Buddhism, Hinduism, and for that matter, the "religion" of atheism no less than the standard American denominations. All these have a "legitimate" place in America. But in some cases, obviously, it is a potential rather than actual status. Only Will Herberg's American triplet—Protestant-Catholic-Jew—represents enough Americans, long enough established, to have gained an institutional position explicitly recognized by the general consensus. And among these, some are more equal than others.

The group of Protestant sects and churches were the most authentic prototype of the Old American Way of Life. Not merely because they represented the predominant religion of the dominant social classes. The personal attitudes and patterns of social and ecclesiastical organization characteristic of Protestantism were in close harmony with liberal doctrines; were, in fact, an important historical source of liberalistic values. American Protestantism was, and is, a loose, open network of voluntaristic sects and denominations with freedom of movement from one to another as men move from village to town, or up the social ladder.

In the view of Protestant America, the freedom of worship

and the privacy of religious conscience are rights of individuals and not of collective entities at all. Religion really resides in the individual and in his direct confrontation of God and God's Word. Church and congregation are, at bottom, social conventions, instruments to help the individual realize religion; they are not the actuality of religion.

Old America therefore finds it natural for social distinctions or other personal considerations to determine which denomination or sect a man belongs to at a particular time and place. To change churches rather frequently during a lifetime is no flaw in piety, for piety is what occurs within the individual himself, irrespective of any particular social framework. Indeed, the ability to be pious in any one of a number of denominations, according to changing circumstances or personal tastes, might almost be considered a positive American trait: it combines complete public mobility with a privacy completely individual in a way very congenial to the American Way of Life.

To be fully and truly assimilated into Old America, one really had to be part of this. Not only Muslims, Hindus, or Buddhists, but Jews and Catholics remained somehow outside. Lacking a Methodist church in a village where they lived, they could not easily find their place in a Baptist congregation instead. If the Presbyterian church were too far away in their town, they could not conveniently go to services in the nearby Congregational church instead. They were not, therefore, part of the most authentic America; and the effect was not limited to the privacy of religion. For, to be shut off from the dominant American churches also meant—especially for Jewish and Catholic New Americans—to be ineligible or restricted in pursuing opportunities the Old Americans regarded as their private business: for example, in exclusive residential areas, clubs, schools, and colleges, and the secure, lucrative top jobs and memberships of America's dominant corporate and financial institutions.

Such an extension of private distinctions from religion into business is nevertheless opposed to the ideal of an open society, and made Old Americans feel vaguely guilty of offending against the American Way. But they noted that immigrant groups were using their own religious privacy for more than the individual practice of faith. They were building collective, secluded enclaves in America: a hierarchical church or a clannish ethnicity, preserving under the principle of separation of church and state a block of Catholic and Jewish minorities who resisted integration into the American Way.

Old America could hardly regard this as within the authentic American tradition; but there was no need to do anything about that. Freedom of religion includes, of course, freedom to have one's own idea of what religion really is. If Catholics regarded religion as inhering essentially in the whole believing community, not the individual communicant, and if Jews really believed their religion to occur in their historic community, not to the isolated individual, then such views were no doubt legitimate in America—though they were certainly not the authentic American Way. The practical consequence might then be summed up in a fleeting reflection that, while social and economic discrimination against religious minorities might, perhaps, be un-American, the Jews and Catholics, in a way, invited such treatment by resisting full Americanization.

A certain ambivalence in the attitude of Old Americans to the assimilation of newcomers was the result. On the one hand, maintaining collective privacies was a regrettable aberration, which must be permitted under the freedom of religion but which one would hope might gradually be overcome. On the other hand, the segregation thereby set up in American life relieved the Old Americans of the pressure to absorb newcomers socially that fully consistent adherence to the ideal of free individual mobility would have demanded of them.

Ambivalent or not, the basic American attitude was to expect and demand the ultimate assimilation and Americanization

48

of all who lived here. Delayed and limited success at any time did not shake confidence in the sure and steady achievement of the goal. The New Americans would all, in the end, become Old Americans like their predecessors.

All, that is, but two: the Jews and the Negroes, for different reasons, were troublesome problems and might well prove to be "unassimilable."

COLOR AND CREED IN OLD AMERICA

Why Negroes could not be assimilated was as obvious as it was discreditable. Race prejudice in America kept them in their place, segregated and subordinate. The ineradicable taint of color marked them off with brutal finality for special, unequal treatment.

With the Jews their religion had a similar effect, but it was neither as obvious nor as obviously discreditable. If there was segregation and subordination of Jews, if they were marked off and discriminated against, a least the source of their troubles was not in theory ineradicable. They could always convert, and if they did not, the consequences they incurred could be said to be chosen by themselves. If there was prejudice, Jews might be said to invite it.

These crude descriptions of the classic Negro and Jewish minority situations are true to this day, but even in regard to Old America they imply strikingly anachronistic attitudes. Since the Civil War at least, Americans have had no right to "keep niggers in their place." In a liberal America, the emancipation from slavery should mean equal opportunity in everything, not only before the law. As for the Jews, there was never a time since the colonies became states when the federal constitution countenanced restrictions on their freedom or opportunities on grounds of religion.

The discrepancies were not however, a simple result of

Americans' failing to abide by their own principles. The whole structure of the Negro and Jewish groups, the net effect of their histories, produced their special fate and destiny with inevitability. Not by accident but by historical necessity, as the Marxists like to say, were these classic minorities chosen for special treatment.

*   *   *

The travail of the American Negro belongs fully, integrally, tragically, and peculiarly to American history. To be an Athenian helot, a medieval serf, an Ottoman slave meant to be degraded and abused not only at the whim but by the established right of the master. These institutions, nonetheless, assumed a bond between lord and servant which left room for affection and loyalty built into the relationship and not depending on the chance of exceptional personal qualities and mutual attraction. For, the institutions of command and obedience were often also institutions of patronage and clienthood. Protection, with all the obligations of care and not merely domination, was the counterpart role that balanced service in many social systems. Rarely, as in America, was this relationship reduced to an institution of simple chattel ownership. If there was kindness and loyalty on either side of the master-slave relation in the Old South, it was hardly the system but rather the human deviations of feeling men and women that created them.

What happened in America, as Stanley Elkins notes, was that those social institutions which primarily form human values, above all the church, were not, as in other cases, involved in forming the master-slave relationship. It was left solely to the political and economic sides of social structures in the Old South to shape that peculiar institution. No ceremonies of homage or pledges of paternal care had any impact on the relationship between master and man. All that counted were the

50

considerations of profitable and effective management which the owner applied to his property. And the governing legal and other defining institutions were largely concerned with supporting the free exercise of owners' rights.

This, as everyone knows, meant—apart from marginal cases of Negro freedmen and some privileged house servants—the total destruction of the Negro family, the loss of all roles that could uphold self-respect and implant a proud identity, and the general exclusion of blacks from all developed culture, whether their own African tradition or that of civilized, literate, white Christian America. It was an unparalleled degradation, deeper and more thorough than that of other slaves; for, in other societies, master and servant were bound to each other by conventions that in principle required emotional and expressive, and not merely rational and calculating, relations between them.

It has been pointed out by Oscar Handlin that in creating its peculiar institution, slaveholding America introduced racial doctrines into its basic system of law and its very vocabulary. The meaning of "slave," a word originally applied to white indentured servants sold for a limited number of years, could not be the same when it also meant captive blacks sold outright in Africa and bought for life in Charleston or Savannah. Terms had to be specified and facts distinguished in order to separate the two situations. A special legal status for blacks turned them into chattel and gave the word "slave" an exclusive racial reference: slaves were blacks, and blacks—notwithstanding freedmen and other exceptions—were by nature slaves.

But, beyond the level of popular stereotypes, slavery penetrated American culture no deeper than the superficial plane of law and legally oriented vocabulary. The sustaining prejudices of the slaveholding system were powerful and comprehensive, covering every possible relationship with blacks, but they remained vulgar prejudices. Apologists for slavery on any literate level could produce no more than theological quibbles or pseudoscientific paradoxes which contributed nothing to either religion or culture. Their whole activity came from no profound concern with religion or culture, but from the unabashed need to defend political and economic positions. The whole syndrome of Negrophobia in America remained, as the sociologists put it, an essentially countermoral phenomenon.

But it was also rooted in the most significant, bloodiest, most critical, and divisive issue that ever stamped its mark upon the American national consciousness. The Civil War and the bitter Reconstruction fixed the patterns of American politics for generations and hardened and perpetuated the irrational hostilities implanted by slavery. The highest and deepest sources of national morality were corrupted. The churches, built on the brotherhood of men and the common fatherhood of God, were organized on color lines by the tacit mutual avoidance of blacks and whites. Jim Crow laws in the South and the hard cake of custom in the North made a mockery of the idea of the open society; a blatant breach of principle politely referred to by Gunnar Myrdal as "*the* American dilemma."

The deepest roots of so powerful a prejudice were imbedded in American sex mores. Masters everywhere tend to follow the Muslim maxim in relation to subjected peoples: "We take their women; they do not take ours." But in America this principle was curdled in the bile of Puritanical sex repression and of a sadomasochistic race abhorrence. The constant fear of servile rebellion bred constant anxiety about black revenge by stealth, particularly by stealthy sex; and it called forth a constant stealthy sexual brutality in reaction and anticipation.

These were habits of thought and feeling that survived Negro emancipation and made the white world they lived in a world of vulgar brutality. They would have found it hard enough in any circumstances to make their way in the testing competition of an open American society. As farmhands from a backward agrarian region, deprived of skills, elementary education, and

52

even, all too frequently, of the inner security arising out of childhood in a stable family, they were ill-equipped for combat under the liberalistic rules of a fair game and no favor. But they were not even admitted to competition.

The way into the real America was open to a Negro only if he could "pass." That left it open only to the most bleached and the most schooled in dissimulation. But the rest, in flat disregard of the American Way, were decreed unassimilable.

*   *   *

The Jewish situation, in contrast, had no roots at all in significant American history. There was no historic national act of Jewish emancipation, for there was never in the history of the federal union a status of Jewish disfranchisement to be overthrown. The minor disabilities Jews suffered under state laws, going back to colonial times, made no impression on the national consciousness since, for one thing, they applied to so few that the subject was negligible.

If, therefore, the Jews remained unassimilable, it was an anachronism more blatant than the persistence of Negro segregation and Negrophobia after the Civil War. A distinct and separate position for the Jewish minority was publicly established—often under conditions of grudging and dubious legitimacy—only in sacrally organized societies, like medieval Christendom or Islam down to our days. Even in secular European states, the persistent, factually ethnic, segregation of unassimilable Jews was an anachronistic effect of an earlier established Jewish status: it was a "relic of the Middle Ages," to use the common expression. But in Europe the emancipation of the Jews was one aspect of revolutions that had scarred many national histories, as deeply and as permanently as the Civil War affected us. In America, where no traditional Jewish status was formally established nor was the revolution at all concerned with the Jewish problem,

53

the unassimilable Jew was doubly anachronistic. He belonged not to our national history but to a realm of religious taboos never formally sanctioned in the American Way of Life or institutionalized by an act of the national consensus.

Negrophobia is imbedded in the bloody soil of our prolonged agony over the slave issue and its never completed resolution, while anti-Semitism has only the shallowest roots in any specifically national, American experience. But just as the color line is a brute fact, so the white man's horror of race mixture is a response of stark, elemental unreason, as arbitrary as a physical fact and equally independent of any justification. Anti-Semitism, in comparison, is the far more profound and serious hatred.

The inequality and segregation of the Negro is merely a defect in our civilization, not a contributory element in our higher culture. In spite of the feeble efforts of pre-Civil War Southern polemicists and recurrent debates over genetic differences, no serious attempt to justify Negro oppression has left a permanent impress upon our intellectual or artistic heritage. One has to examine the cruder operations of the subconscious to find the remote and devious influences of Negro suppression upon American creativity. Fundamentally, positive Negro-hatred remains nothing more than an element of vulgarity in American culture.

The "Jewish problem," as liberal Jews or Gentiles discover with great difficulty, is quite a different matter. Only against severe inner resistance can they appreciate how intricately the Jewish-Christian conflict is involved in the higher culture which they both share—and which subtly sets them one against the other. Anti-Jewish attitudes are not merely vulgar lapses among Gentiles, especially Christians; though they can be that too. They are woven into the warp and woof of all that is most precious and intimate in Western civilization. The symbols of the eschatological war between Church and Synagogue adorn cathedrals and inform the catechism with high dramatic tension. The awe and dread of Ahasuerus, of the Cain people, have contributed to the beauty, the sublimity, the pathos of the whole range of Western religion, folklore, poetry, drama, music, art. It is in Shakespeare's Shylock, Dickens' Fagin, and the Passion Play; it is in Chaucer, in Grimm's fairy tales, in the great chorales of Bach—and even in the queerly ambivalent Jew-apotheosis of Leon Bloy.

If our national history made Negroes unassimilable in America, a deeply rooted religious tradition had the same effect upon the Jews. But religious differences did not have similar consequences for Christian minorities who questioned certain values of the dominant WASP establishment.

It is true that religion provided a shelter of collective privacy under which many ethnic traditions found a certain protection in America. The Catholic Church served as a focus for Irish patriotism, for Italian folk culture, and for instruction in the French, Polish, and Spanish languages and traditions. The Lutheran Church allowed Germans and Swedes to foster their ethnic consciousness and traditions in America. But none except the Jews are so marked off that what is enforced, or willingly maintained, under the shelter of religious freedom is in actuality the persistence of a single historical nationality.

All other immigrant churches, while helping to preserve elements of various ethnic cultures, also served as a zone of partial merger and assimilation of the original ethnic entities. Each Christian Church fostered not one but several ethnicities. Irish, French, Poles, and Latin Americans were all Catholics, and Swedes and Germans both were Protestants. Not only was the most intimate association, that of intermarriage, permitted between them by the church; the common religion facilitated it.

These churches, moreover, always encompassed Americans not included in a tight ethnic ghetto but forming part of the real America. For, all major immigrant Christian churches were represented in the Old American stock that ruled the several states and helped form the original American consensus since colonial and revolutionary times. It is a fact of American life that Old Americans like Orestes A. Brownson or Clare Booth Luce could convert, let us say, from Presbyterianism to Catholicism without breaking contact with the nuclear American community and entering into a social segregation. This, in principle, opens the way for lace-curtain Irish and other highly polished upper-class immigrant Catholics to participate with no, or insignificant, restrictions in the general American cultural and religious mobility.

It is equally a fact of American, no less than of Jewish life anywhere that precisely this possibility is precluded for anyone who continues to be identified as a Jew. "Our Crowd" of Jewish plutocrats and philanthropists, notables in every business or public activity that could gain renown in liberal America, never broke into the real American inner circle. Not, at any rate, unless they converted like August Belmont; in which case the usual objections to Jews, such as their alleged vulgarity, ostentation, and general pushiness (of which he was a prime example), were eventually set aside. But failing conversion, no Jew could break out of the ethnic reservation. For any Gentile to convert to Judaism, no less in America than anywhere else, meant to break his old ties and enter into the Jewish segregation.

There was only one ethnic group, only one historic nationality in the Jewish church: it was the Jewish people. German Jews, Russian Jews, and Jews of Spanish-Portuguese antecedents were, no doubt, aware of their differing backgrounds and inclined to stress their importance. Other Americans rarely made such distinctions among Jews. In the end the effect of moving to America was to consolidate among all Jewish immigrants, except those who "passed" by the door of conversion, a common *Jewish* identity. The fusion that took place between Spanish-Portuguese, German, and Russian Jews was like the emergence of a common Polish or Czechoslovak national consciousness among peasant immigrants to America who in the Old Country had identified with their village, province, or region rather than the nation-state. What did not take place among Jews was the further fusion that grouped ethnics into large blocs of Catholic Irish-Italian-Polish or Protestant German-Swedish or Scotch-Irish-Anglo-Saxon Americans, blurring the original unitary national identification.

The "melting pot" theory was never a precise description of what happened in America. Thanks to the immigrant ghetto, the general looseness of social requirements, and the collective shelter provided by religious freedom, the European New Immigration was not transformed into a uniformly fused mass in the second or third generation. American experience has taught us to distinguish between "assimilation" and "acculturation": between a social amalgamation that enables the individual to move freely through the range of a society and a cultural initiation that only introduces him to its symbols of communication and other conventions. Cultural absorption usually begins sooner and progresses farther than social. But, despite the rapid acculturation of immigrants, our American melting pot is still full of lumps organized around disjoined cultural as well as social nuclei. These are generally new clusters, formed by dim forces of attraction and repulsion out of elements of the old, gradually dissolving, ethnic groups. We may have Catholic or Lutheran ethnoreligious groupings that go to make up our common America, or even Slavic-Catholic, Latin-Catholic, German-Scandinavian-Lutheran and other, similar amalgams. But we do not, in general, have a rigid persistence of the original groups who came here.

Jews and Negroes—together with other odd men out, like American Indians, Mexicans or Puerto Ricans, and Orientals—remain more or less isolated above the influx that produced these amalgamations. The lines that mark out Jews and Negroes remain distinct—and effective. They have been able to "pass" only as individuals, through a harsh and usually demeaning process of conversion or dissimulation; and the barriers against individuals "passing" in any other way establish invidious discriminations against the group. They have not yielded to or been absorbed in the trend towards the reduction of old groups and their fusion and coalescence in new and larger groupings, formed with cognate ethnic entities. There *are* no such cognate entities for Jews and Negroes, because the racial line and the religious bar which mark them off from other Americans are in both cases unique and distinct.

*　　*　　*

Anyone known to have Negro blood is a Negro; anyone born Jewish is a Jew, unless converted. Anyone who marries a Negro is cut out of the lily-white community, and may or may not be accepted among Negroes. Anyone who marries a Jew cannot easily bring him, together with the family, into the community of Gentiles without conversion; and such a person can only truly enter the Jewish community by conversion.

What history lies behind these distinctions and exclusions, as firm and clear as they are arbitrary? The American color line is easily understood as a product of the history of American slavery. The history behind the religious barriers that define who is a Jew—including no-longer-believing Jews—is more complex, ecumenical, and hard to grasp.

The Jew, whether he believes or not, is a product of Judaism and its peculiar history. Like the other monotheistic faiths that sprang from it, Judaism, as Yehezkel Kaufmann argued, was necessarily a conversionist religion. If it failed to bring into the fold many peoples, as did the daughter religions Christianity and Islam, it was because of one reason only: Judaism was the religion of a defeated people. To convert to Judaism meant to accept penalties which, in most centuries of the long Jewish travail from Greco-Roman to modern times, were tangible, painful, and legally enforced. At all times it has meant accepting a status of social subjection or, at best, depreciation.

Under such circumstances conversion to Judaism was only rarely undertaken by whole groups; and in the course of history many of those later separated from the Jews, if originally sectarian like the Christians, or faded into oblivion like the Khazars, the Jewish kingdom of Adiabene, and the Jewish tribes of Arabia or North Africa.

There were exceptional cases. Most conversions were individual: rare men or women who were ready to join a people whose millennial Exile was institutionally recognized in their own culture, as well as that of the Gentile world. Converts were necessarily few; and—as in the case of Jews who converted —the act effectively removed them from one and brought them into another ethnic community. Judaism thus remained the religion of a single people, the Jews. When Jews came to America, the ethnic community they preserved through the collective privacy of religion was also that of a single historic people, the Jewish people.

With conversion the sole avenue for leaving, as well as entering, the community of Jews, all those born Jews remained Jews by social definition even if they no longer believed in Judaism. A religion they no longer held was the effective barrier which prevented such Jews from being accepted as real Americans. Even though a long national history and a rich culture (and not merely thin existentialist rationalizations of a condition of oppression) stood behind this ethnic identity, how could one define values adequate to express and justify the segregation of unbelieving American Jews? Or, for that matter, if church is truly separated from state in America, what can justify the unassimilability of those Americans who believe in the Torah? Why is their separation absolute, final, and not subject to their

59

own option, when Christian immigrants who differ with the prevailing ideas and habits of the real, Old Americans are only kept in relative, provisional, and more or less voluntary separation?

ACCULTURATED, BUT UNASSIMILABLE

If religion is a final bar to the assimilation of Jews, why not of Catholics, for example, in a dominantly Protestant America? The conflict of values between Catholics and Protestants is in some respects far more acute than between Jews and Protestants; though in other respects less so. Are there then some aspects of culture which close off social contacts more than others?

Between Protestants and Catholics in America, there is consensus on at least one point. Even though religion is completely free and private, and all religious beliefs or unbeliefs must be tolerated, it hardly needs to be stated that America is really a Christian country.

The situation in America and in all secularized Western countries is that the Church is dispossessed of the control of law and politics, as well as literature and philosophy. In good part, this revolution was the work of the emergent nation-state and, in part, of the cosmopolitan brotherhood of humanist intellectuals. The latter challenged the Church on its own universal grounds, setting up reason as the organon and mankind as the historical tribunal of ultimate truth. The nations, on the other hand, revolting against ecumenical dominion, pitted the concrete truth of their individual experience against all universal pretensions.

What the nations achieved was, therefore, a division in the realm of culture. Their history was for each of them the essential source and the touchstone of authenticity for the part of culture that expressed individuality and immediate experience. Art, literature, the consciousness of history, and the collective life-style became historical, national values. But a common tradition of ultimate intellectual and ethical values was shared by the European family of nations, and each rested its individuality upon this universal basis.

The general values of Western civilization derived from religion and science. Secular humanism and scientific enlightenment most significantly affected the "instrumental" aspects of Western life: technology, government, political economy, and other institutions of social management. The fundamental emotional and moral values by which individuals lived were still derived from religious tradition; that is, they were Christian.

This was true even of a country like the United States of America, which from birth established its major institutions on the post-Christian, secular foundations of British liberalism and the French Enlightenment. De Tocqueville concluded that the separation of church and state had lent religion a broader social influence in America than it exercised in those countries where a Church was established.

We have already noted the powerful impact of multisectarian Protestantism upon American ideas of social organization, on its standards of morality, and on what Max Weber called "the economic ethic." This specific religious tradition was equally effective with British Deism and French Enlightenment in forming the liberal political tradition that has been central to our national identity since the Revolution. Our broad ideal of an open society, with associations voluntarily entered into by the free choice of individuals and forming a pluralistic system sustained by, and sustaining, the free mobility of individuals, thus expresses in a unique historical combination certain Western religious and secular ideas originally proposed as universally applicable.

The practical effect of the ideas of voluntaristic, pluralistic liberalism is to deny social doctrines essentially related to Catholicism. The Roman Church has always held that it is the duty of the state to enforce and of society to be ruled by the true belief—that is, the Catholic doctrine as finally enunciated under the sanction of the Pope. This implies, of course, the suppression of false beliefs. The sectarian Protestant and the humanist idea of religious tolerance is nonetheless tolerated by Catholic doctrine when the Church may have to depend on toleration itself, as is often the case in modern times. But a nation-state committed by its history to such principles stands in direct opposition to basic Catholic values.

For Jews, on the other hand, a secular political system affords the opportunity to participate in the public life and the national history of their host-country. When religion is defined as a private affair, much seems for the first time to be opened up to the Jews that was previously denied them. As a result, Jews accept far more readily than do Catholics some major established features of the American Way of Life.

The Catholics would like to persuade America that the Constitution not only permits but should encourage public support of a variety of churches and church schools, even if this involves publicly sponsored segregation between one group of Americans and another. They feel that the rule against an established church need not mean that *no* church should get public support, but that *all* should get *equal* support. Whether or not the language of the Bill of Rights bears such an interpretation, it obviously challenges the usual conception of the American Way of Life. To give formal recognition to permanently segregated religious groups would contradict the most authentically American ideal of religious social organization: the sectarian-Protestant pattern of free, open, voluntaristic sects and denominations.

There is no such clearcut Jewish resistance to the dominant consensus on the question of the kind of social organization appropriate for exercising religious freedom in America. The Jews, as a body, offer no third conception of their own as a challenge to the Catholics and Protestants.

62

In some respects, the prevailing tendency among American Jews is to be more "Protestant" than the Protestants themselves. Protestant enthusiasm for the secular public school system, a major expression of the strict doctrine of separating church and state, was never apparent until the first wave of Catholic mass immigration. In the face of the segregated parochial school, locking in immigrant differences, the public school began to seem an important instrument of Americanization. But, even today, it is Jewish organizations and civil rights groups who most consistently favor the completely secular, religiously neutral public school. They often find themselves defending the basic Protestant position against Protestant infringements, such as the observance of Christian ceremonies in the schools.

On the other hand, there is a growing tendency for some American Jews, particularly among the Orthodox, to lean towards the Catholic rather than the Protestant model for religious social organization. One finds increasing support for the idea of Jewish "parochial" schools and a readiness to think of a plurality of established, or at least recognized, American religions—including, of course, the Jewish religion.

While wavering cautiously and defensively between the rival Protestant and Catholic conceptions, the Jews are prominently represented in efforts to persuade everyone concerned that not religious differences but the "consensus" among all parties is most significant and authentically American. In that "consensus" the Jews, naturally, include their own basic beliefs, and so lay claim to being, also, authentically American.

The divisive potential in this area of American social relations is evidently disturbing enough to make any formula generally attractive that would construct a positive consensus where no more actually exists than the negative agreement to disagree. Consequently, the Jews, not involved fully on the side of either party and, at bottom, in fear of both, have had great success in their persuasive endeavors; and they have been well rewarded themselves. Where else in the world is it so common to speak

63

(not only among Jews but among Christians) of the Judeo-Christian ethic, the Judeo-Christian tradition, or the Judeo-Christian foundations of our national Way of Life?

*   *   *

The implication of the phrase is, as already noted, that Jews are not only entitled to toleration, like Buddhists or Muslims; their religious values are purportedly an integral part of the American Heritage. By no stretch of the imagination could anyone conceive of Buddhists or Muslims making such a claim.

There is, of course, a closer historical relationship between Christianity and Judaism than between Buddhism, or even Islam, and Christianity. But we are considering something much more specific than this: the slogan of a "Judeo-Christian tradition" implies that Judaism is intimately related to the American Way of Life, and not just to Christianity. The fact that Christianity, like Islam, sprang from a Jewish root, and that Jews remained in closer contact with Christendom throughout its development than did Muslims, is true, but pointless in this connection. The implied claim of a Jewish share in the American Way of Life is certainly more pertinent, but on the other hand, false.

It is true that American Protestantism, in its reaction against "Papism," was fond of recalling Hebrew origins. But the point at issue really is this: to what extent does authentic Judaism provide principles for social organization in Christian countries and particularly in America? Or, to put it more bluntly: to what extent is the Jewish community essential to the American Way of Life, or the way of life of any Christian country? Are they so integrally and intimately a part of it anywhere that their absence would be inconceivable or radically alter its character?

We need only put these questions to be certain of their answers. In all Christian countries, and in America too, the basic Christian tradition which still fundamentally affects attitudes regards the Jews as a people rejected of God. They must eventually disappear when God lets them be reconciled to Him. In the meantime they exist as people under a ban: they should not be molested, but they remain essentially alien in the Christian world. As for their doctrine, it is a rejected doctrine, superseded by the New Testament.

Given these attitudes, how could the Jewish collectivity or the Jewish doctrine, as authentically developed by themselves, have shaped the way of life of America, or any Christian country? Is it any wonder that Jews are marked by their caution and reserve, and fear to assert a special Jewish viewpoint on any issue of American social organization? Whatever influence "Hebrew ideas" had on American social organization, it could not have come from the rejected doctrine of Judaism. In fact it came solely through Protestant variants of Christianity. As for the Jews themselves, it is hard to see how their absence from any Christian country, including America, would alter its way of life in any essential.

*　　*　　*

Catholics may oppose established principles of the American Way more than Jews care or dare to do. But they share other values, fundamental to the American Way, that are impossible for Jews to share in the same way: they are Christians, as America is basically Christian. For this reason, and not only because Catholicism comprises many ethnic groups, both immigrant and long-settled, while Judaism comprises only one, Catholics are basically assimilable in America, while Jews are not.

This is not simply a matter of conflicting beliefs. What makes a Jew unassimilable to a Christian society is not simply his

65

rejection of Christian dogmas like the Trinity or the divine Christ; nor, on the other hand, is the Jew's faith in his revealed Law and Rabbinic tradition the whole problem. Unitarians, Universalists, old-time Deists might deny the Trinity and revere Jesus only as the first of the prophets without the least effect on their status as real, fully authentic Americans. They constitute, in fact, a good part of the Founding Fathers of our national history and a major element among the innermost American elite today. Even atheism is no social disqualification in itself for one born a Christian. But Jews of precisely the same opinions remain outside this charmed circle. So, too, a Jew who no longer believes in Revelation or lives by the Talmud in no way overcomes the essential difference that excludes him from a Christian society. However, once he converts to any Christian faith, a door is opened for the process, or the succession of sometimes dilatory processes, that may successfully assimilate him.

In the extreme, minimal case of the atheistic Jew, we can isolate the ultimate difference that makes Jews unassimilable. There are values such a Jew cannot share which are part of the childhood patrimony of an atheistic native Christian. There are residual values he shares with other Jews that are strange or repugnant to men born Gentile. These are not clear and fixed distinctions, but they are effective; decisively so.

Jews under the pressure of an environment hostile, at bottom, to their traditional culture are susceptible to self-hatred. This acculturates them to Gentile anti-Semitism in their response to various Jewish values—which may differ in different countries. In Russia it is common for acculturated Jews to abhor the practice of circumcision as a "cannibalistic rite," while in America it is the Jewish national identity formally acknowledged in Soviet culture that is repugnant and disturbing to many over-Americanized Jews. But even in this case, without conversion or some other effective means of "passing" into a

Gentile condition there always remain residual, mainly emotional—or, as the psychologists say, "affective"—aspects of the Jewish subculture which set the Jew apart. A Jewish atheist in America or Comsomol in Russia will always find natural, or even appealing, some features of the private Jewish subculture that he would mock, scorn, or resent if he were a Gentile atheist or Comsomol.

The same is true on the other side as well. No matter how much of the Christian-tinged public culture a Jew may absorb; whether he simply adopts their Christmas tree and enjoys their liturgical music or also succumbs to their anti-Jewish clichés in judgment of his own heritage: there remain emotional experiences he has not shared and cannot really stomach. He has never taken in the blood and flesh of Jesus in communion, nor has the Crucifixion ever been absorbed into his identity as a trauma of Salvation. A Christian-born atheist may have lost his belief in these matters; but he is not likely to pick up the revulsion and distaste of the born Jew for such rituals. However incongruously, and in spite of the sincerest efforts at sophisticated tolerance, a Jew reacts to basic emotional aspects of the Christian tradition as to paganism and idolatry. The stern, monotheistic, purist rationalism of his ancestral faith remains with the emancipated, freethinking Jew—and it sustains his irriducible unassimilability.

*   *   *

The minimal American Jew, like the American Negro, is so deeply acculturated to the American Way that his own identity is undermined and confused. Even the more fully committed American Jews, like modern Jews in all Western countries, have identified with their country, its culture and national history, to an extent unknown before the modern period. When the dominant culture which they have largely adopted defines them openly or tacitly as unassimilable, this produces for them, as for the American Negro, problems unknown to Jews in earlier times.

There is an element of conflict and resistance at all times in the relations of any minority with its social environment. Peculiarly complex and sometimes acute problems arise when the minority is frustrated in its identification with a dominant culture that it largely and profoundly, though never fully, accepts.

III.   The Confusion of Identities

As unassimilated and probably unassimilable minorities, Jews and Negroes stood together in the tacit register of excluded breeds and classes maintained by the Old Americans. But the ultimate grounds of their exclusion were poles apart. The way they were treated by other Americans was reflected in their own self-image: here, too, certain common traits combined with striking differences. The full implication of the differences only became apparent in the present, new era, when the moral foundations and assumptions of the Old America have been thoroughly shaken.

Not their differences but the fact that both seemed unassimilable was uppermost in Old American awareness of Jews and Negroes. Excluded socially, both were conventionally assumed to be included culturally, at least sufficiently so to protect the value consensus upon which the American Way was based.

I have already noted who produced the serious, universal values of the American Way of Life. It is no longer as acceptable to stress this fact as it was during the vogue of Know-Nothingism, nativism, or Nordic supremacism. But any descriptive sociology would have to concede that our fundamental *mores,* from the Puritan code to the Protestant ethic, from the ideal of rugged individualism to the Constitution and Bill of Rights, still derive primarily from the WASP "majority." This common American culture may continually need to be accepted, acquiesced in, or submitted to by everybody. But the daily plebiscite that ratifies our national creed is, like every plebiscite, an enforced choice between alternatives which the electorate did not create. The alternatives are presented to them ready-made by their leaders.

I have also noted the effect of referring to the minorities' value systems as "subcultures." It implies values distinct from but subordinate to the dominant values, and included in and essentially harmonious with the culture of the country as a whole. It suggests that the "subcultures" add no more than trivial, entertaining, essentially amiable touches to the basic, common, true American culture. It conveys the tacit assumption that serious, universal values that are held by the minorities are either fully derived from the dominant culture or suitably acculturated to it, if they become naturalized in America.

Observers of the American Negro and Jewish subcultures who followed these leads tended to concentrate on such values as come under the heading of "folkways." The Negro subculture was then described as a matter of jazz rhythms, blue notes and blues harmonies, spirituals and folk songs, fish fries and funerals, and other touches of local color with which the Negro subcommunity, from Basin Street to Harlem, embroidered the basic fabric of American culture. The Jewish subculture, in the same vein, was thought to consist in a characteristic turn of wit and humor, derived from the East European *shtetl,* and distilled and blended for the American market in successive haunts of the Jewish subcommunity, from the immigrant ghetto to the borscht belt to suburbia and exurbia, or it showed itself in relative immunity to alcoholism and relative addiction to higher education among Jews, and so on.

The obvious difficulty in taking this tack with regard to the Jews was the fact that they were defined as a minority by the formal criterion of their religion. They were segregated precisely because of the most serious and intimate of values. But the suggestion of conflict rather than full accord in this sphere

70

could be, and was, defended against by various devices, apologetic and adaptive.

There was above all, the doctrine (far from new among Western Jewries, each with reference to its own country) of the intrinsic harmony between Judaism and Americanism. This was expressed, as noted in the preceding chapter, in the widely used catchword of the "Judeo-Christian tradition" or in the notion that Judaism was one of three specially accredited religions—along with Catholicism and Protestantism—among which all Americans are conventionally divided, and to one of which all are expected to belong.

The apologetic function of such ideas, when used by Jews, is clear. They arise from the tacit recognition that it is not enough merely to separate church from state and make religion a private affair in order to gain equal access for Jews to all social, economic, or even political opportunities. Religion remains *de facto* a qualifying criterion for many secular activities. Consequently, if one succeeds in gaining acceptance for Judaism as one of the specially accredited American religions, the restrictions Jews experience may perhaps lose their force, if not at once then by gradual attrition.

The popular success of these notions depends on a dilution of religious faith, as certain theologians, both Jewish and Christian, complain. Arthur A. Cohen points out that the "myth of the Judeo-Christian tradition" flourished historically in periods of growing unbelief. It gains a tone of urgency today when both Jewish and Christian "religionists" seek to meet the threat of secularism by borrowing incongruously from each other's antithetical religious attitudes. As for Will Herberg's three accredited American religions, Herberg gloomily confessed that they rest on the common base of an idolatrous religion of Americanism, whose blighting prevalence had long been bewailed and condemned by Reinhold Niebuhr.

One effect of these apologetic ideas, and of the other adjustments Jews make in their religious folkways and organization to conform to WASP patterns, has been to confuse severely the Jews' sense of their historical identity. In the more advanced forms of the American Jewish church, adaptation to Protestantism has meant a great dilution of authentic individuality as well as pious commitment. Not only by intent but in fact, American Judaism can become so determinedly American that it is a fair and natural question on what basis some Jews still remain unassimilated. That they and others still consider them Jews may well appear to be quite arbitrary.

Nevertheless, no matter how nominal their Jewishness, such Jews, unless they are converted, *do* remain unassimilated. American Jews (unlike Western and Central European Jews in pre-Hitler days) had until recently a remarkably low rate of intermarriage with Gentiles. Their patterns of residence and occupation—again, until recently—were relatively narrow, segregated, and special; and this remained true in the so-called "areas of second settlement" beyond the immigrant ghetto, after a rapid rise to the middle class was well under way. The wealthy Jew, if unconverted, had an honored place in the Jewish community, whenever he wished to claim it, but was shut out of the inner circle of his Christian class-peers by a barrier as firm as it was intangible.

Not being a Christian, he could not be a real American. Even in its most denatured and washed-out form, American Judaism was dimly perceived by real Americans as antithetical to vital parts of their own, basically Christian civilization. In this, their instinct was, of course, correct.

But in what specific ways was American Judaism antithetical to Christian-based real Americanism? This was a question rigorously suppressed by all well-meaning Gentiles, and answered only by anti-Semites out of their demonological folklore. American Jews, like other Western Jews, sometimes rejected not only the lying propaganda against them but also the whole project of defining their identity out of the antithesis to their environment. But then they were left with no adequate cultural justification for remaining permanently separate, unassimilated.

As for the Negro, no one could doubt that he was an American—precisely in the sense the Jew was not, and could not be. His piety, his normative religious culture were not only Christian but American Christian. He might be a kind of pariah and belong to a closed caste; but he had a fixed place in American society—and in no other—given his native Americanism. One of the constant drives of American Jewry is the vain hope to gain, by the naturalization of Judaism in this country, unquestioned acceptance for themselves in this one area where American Negroes have it.

But it makes for an even deeper confusion of identity when the Negro, who is nothing if not American, remains unassimilable. What help is it to be American if one is shut out of the "open society" that is the real America? Increasingly, this intractable contradiction has been diagnosed in terms of an identity crisis of the American Negro. James Baldwin inveighed against the white man's myth which had created out of white prejudice a meaningless Negro identity for the black American. In place of the white "myth of the Negro past," some blacks now sought a real past all their own which would make their identity meaningful.

Such an historically rooted identity, rising out of a reclaimed authentic black culture, would unite the Negro community as an effective political and economic force. It would restore pride, discipline, self-respect, and their very manhood to Negro men. By closing their own ranks, the black Afro-Americans would also break dialectically into the open society that had been closed to Negro Americans.

In all this, there was frequent implicit, and often explicit, reference to what Jews had achieved in America, and how it

73

was believed they had achieved it. Communal discipline, a proud historical self-consciousness, the exercise of power—these, black militants preached, were the methods of the Jews in breaking out of the immigrant ghetto to the heights of American society. Underlying it all was the powerful sense of their separate identity which was the Jews' secret weapon.

Much of this is the Negro's myth about the contemporary American Jew. In fact, the Jew today is about as confused in his identity, as communally undisciplined, and, in his own way, as detached from historical roots as the American Negro. It is a striking fact that the source for much existentialist black analysis of the current Negro problem is Jean Paul Sartre's account of the modern Jew as a fiction created by the malevolent imagination of anti-Semites. Shallow and unreal as this description was, it was nevertheless based on intimate observation of native Jews in France, a collective body whose individual members in many cases see no reason for their identification except the anti-Jewish prejudice of Frenchmen.

The emancipated Western Jew tends to become what the emancipated Negro initially is: an arbitrary collective category with no intrinsic meaning for its individual members, but imposed upon them by outside forces; a social fact detached from any identifying culture and history; an existence without essence; a Sartrean existential fate. But such a pointless fate has not usually been one that Jews could live with even in the slim conviction of Sartrean "authenticity." There was no dialectical struggle in the successful adjustment of Jews to Western society, as Negro militants imagine, but at most a struggle for the right to be submerged. The modern Jew was nevertheless initially formed by his history and by all those powers black militants invoke in repudiating *their* initial condition: by an ethnic identity, culture, and history; by an organized community and independent communal consensus.

The differences between Jew and Negro grow more apparent

the more we look to the past: to plantation slavery and the medieval ghetto. Today they are increasingly obscured, because the Negro is reaching for the benefits of the Jewish position while the Jew, for his part, hopes to attain the relative advantage of the Negro position. In his anxiety to be as purely American as the Negro is, the Jew reduces his ideological resistance as nearly as possible to the level of a mythic variant of general American culture. He thus weakens his independent consensus. The Negro, hoping to attain such a rise in status as the Jew has accomplished since immigration, heightens his opposition as nearly as possible to the level of ideology. His new combativeness fosters what Jews avoid: a community organized around its own consensus, independent of the standards of the general American community.

IDEOLOGICAL AND SOCIAL MINORITIES

The classic Jewish and Negro minorities were outgroups in America both in terms of social status and of culture. But the primary source of Negro segregation was their social position, while for Jews it was the ancient culture they were identified with. Without too much violence to the facts, one could use them to illustrate two ideal types in polar opposition, the purely social and the purely ideological minority.

Both types are in some degree of conflict with the dominant culture. Where subjection is essentially social, the minority subculture develops a folklore of its own which represents what I may call a *mythic* variant of the dominant culture. There is no open, ideological opposition. The implicit challenge and conflict is veiled or even subconscious. An *ideological* minority, on the other hand, is constituted from the outset by a direct clash of values.

Where a conflict of values is no more than mythic, both groups involved live within a consensus fully defined by the same ideology. Minorities who suffer restriction or deprivation under the established norms can ease the rigid pressure of the rules by applying wit and humor and other subterfuges by which disciplines can be relaxed or evaded without openly breaking them. But where the conflict is ideological and begins with an open clash, a radically different problem exists.

The logic of the situation initially requires a victory of one side over the other, completely suppressing it. If this cannot be achieved, a contract of peaceful coexistence may be arranged between the opposed groups, with each solely governed, within that limit, by its own distinct consensus. An ideological minority represents a third alternative, in which the victorious group absorbs but is not able to submerge totally its ideological rival. The minority is then *tolerated*: that is, it lives by its own distinct consensus within limits not mutually contracted but defined unilaterally by the consensus of the dominant ideology.

The kind of group whose conflict with the dominant culture remains essentially mythic includes such types as serfs, slaves, pariahs, and other suppressed classes. Fear of servile rebellion underlies the attitude of master classes towards them. When rebellion occurs and the masters resort to violence to repress it, their aim is to put the lower classes back, or keep them chained down, in their proper place—*within* the society. When there is peace between the masters and their bound men, the servile subcommunity "knows its place" as defined by the dominant culture, and vents its resentment only in the guarded, arcane forms of humor, games, folklore, subgroup slang or coded talk, and other subcultural expressions. The masters, for their part, act the part of patron and care for the men bound to their person and domain as their own people.

The kind of group whose conflict with the dominant culture is ideological includes such types as religious sects, radical factions, and colonies of foreign devils or merchant adventurers. Fear of conquest or subversion underlies the attitude of the dominant community towards them. If the threat seems so imminent that the dominant group resorts to violence, its aim is to expel or exterminate the enemy, or convert them to the ruling ideology: in any case, to wipe them out as a subculture or subcommunity. When peace and tolerance prevail between dominant and dissident ideologies, the minority lives partly outside the consensus of the main community and is often regarded as in some degree alien. On the other hand, being loosely attached and needing every advantage, such groups may use their greater mobility to reach relatively high social status, within the limits of their freedom. Not being fully within society, they are not chained to fixed positions in it.

An ideological minority has its own intellectuals who function essentially within its own independent consensus. They may be ideologues or preachers, revolutionaries or apostles, prophets, philosophers or priests, rabbis or dervishes or gurus, but what is common to all is their authentic relationship to the minority they belong to. They depend for the exercise of their proper role upon it, and it depends on them and on their proper performance of their role.

A minority defined socially, with no more than a mythic subculture, usually does not but may occasionally include intellectuals, but in that case their role is to serve the master class. They are essentially marginal men, leaning more to the dominant society and culture than to their own.

The intellectual function is imperative for ideological minorities since they are, in essence, an opposition to the dominant culture. Intellectuals, of course, form the spear-point of this attack and man the defenses of the minority against the ideological assaults of the dominant culture. The morale of the group, upon which its survival fundamentally depends, requires continual, demonstrably effective activity of its intellectual class.

An independent consensus of its own is another inherent requirement for the functioning and the very existence of any

77

ideological group. The relations of such a group with the majority that tolerates it are necessarily unstable. Simply to maintain a balance, let alone win over or win against the majority, the minority needs to manage itself constantly and to manage its contacts with the majority with discipline and care. There is an irreducible political element in the social structure of an ideological minority. It cannot maintain itself with a mythic subculture that does no more than express the specific shared experiences of the group and articulate their private communications. It needs a method for determining a consensus, formal or informal, in order to act in concert and manage its responses to the challenges constantly arising within its tolerated sphere of freedom.

*　　　*　　　*

These are, of course, abstractions. One should not expect Jews or Negroes to conform fully to either ideal type. It is far more likely that elements of both types should be found in the situation of any long-established minority.

The medieval ghetto limited the functions open to Jews so severely that they have been classed by some scholars as pariahs, not only as a sect. When the European Jews were emancipated, or they immigrated to the New World, it required more than tolerance, in the view of Gentiles, in order to absorb them. There was a job of social rehabilitation and uplift to be done as well.

So, too, the Negro position under American slavery, clearly rooted as it was in a brutal social oppression, developed its cultural, and almost ideological, distinctions. Negroes might be Christians, but they were segregated in Negro churches. This could not remain without effect, at least upon ritual, and potentially upon doctrine as well.

Allowing for such reservations, American Negroes were

nevertheless as nearly as possible a case of the subcommunity with a purely mythic subculture, while American Jews were a subcommunity whose subculture was, at bottom, ideologically distinct as well. The enslaved Negroes became Christians and practically forgot, with rare exceptions, that they were ever anything but American. The free, unattached Jews rose rapidly in wealth and position to the limit permitted by tolerance, but they remained unconverted and never really forgot their historic origins. African reminiscences in the Negro's subculture chiefly served to ease the discomforts his American values imposed upon him. Jewish traditions, no matter how attenuated, never ceased to set Jews at odds with certain basic values shared by all other Americans.

The distinction carries over into other areas primarily related to culture, namely, the role of artists and intellectuals and the function of a consensus in the community. The enslaved blacks could and did create a distinctive style in music, theater, and crafts, but they could not create an ethnic literature. Their subculture provided them with the means of semisecret communication and private understanding, a grapevine to pass along news of events affecting them all, and an underground railroad to move runaways to freedom—but not an effectively functioning communal consensus.

Of all the fields of culture, the plastic arts, music, theater are least identified with authentic Jewishness. Jews readily picked up and put off art and music forms wherever they went. In this respect, as Leonard Bernstein's tango number in *Candide* has it, they are "easily assimilated." But what they always kept and continually created were their own books.

Jewish culture has been, and remains, essentially a book culture. As an ideological minority, traditional Jews not only expressed themselves but organized themselves through the word. This implies a peculiarly significant role for the creators of the Jewish literary tradition.

79

Jewish literature was the code and lawbook by which most of a Jew's life, as an individual, was lived. Before the secular revolutions, Jewish communities in all Christian and Muslim lands were separate and autonomous. They bowed to Gentile norms only in marginal, mainly business contacts between their colony and the host society. Internally, the community governed itself to a greater or lesser degree by the centuries-old legal tradition of the Talmud, of which the rabbis were legitimate judges and interpreters.

No general hierarchy like that of the Roman Church disciplined these self-governing institutions, but a common, living, legal, ethical, and religious tradition integrated them in a highly effective, though loosely articulated consensus. The antique Hebrew-Aramaic national language was the universal medium for official, legal communication and for private, commercial transactions between widely distant Jews, and supported the consensus that united them.

Under such circumstances, the several Gentile laws and many different sovereignties which Jews acknowledged did not divide them fundamentally. Differences in Jewish culture arising from this source remained largely mythic, and did not seriously threaten Jewish unity as an ideological group. The universal Jewish consensus, however loosely structured, determined which outside influences had a general effect upon Jewish culture, which produced a tolerated local or regional variant in Jewish customs—and which were decisively rejected.

Nor were the varying social circumstances and economic pursuits of the widely dispersed Jews able to produce ideological conflicts within the consensus of Jewish culture. The scholar Louis Finkelstein may be able to illuminate Talmudic passages by theorizing that the Pharisees represented the class interests of Judean peasants and Jerusalem small traders and artisans. But what is far more striking, even when Jews lived in their own land as a full society and not a minority, was the success of those folk intellectuals, the Pharisees, in imposing their own sectarian ideas and ritual taboos upon the whole people. Certainly in the Diaspora the consensus that united Jews was decisively affected by the normative tradition of their intellectual class, the rabbis. This is what Jews adhered to and identified themselves by, whatever their differences arising from class, status, or the influence of divergent environments.

*   *   *

In another respect the difference between ideological and social minorities, even as ideal types, is limited: in their sense of history. Croce was basically correct in considering as historic only that which man has freely, rationally, actively created. Only an ideological group, not a group living by a merely mythic culture, can be creative freely, rationally, actively. The creations of a nonideological, purely social group are repressed, nonrational, and passively reactive. But, on the other hand, to be a minority is also to be restricted in one's scope for free, rational activity. Thus, an ideological minority must have a sense of history inherent in its ideology, but one restricted by its minority status. Its advantage over a purely social minority in this respect is only relative.

That enslaved American Negroes could have no real sense of their own history is all too obvious. This remains true even if one makes all needed revisions in our description of the subculture of Negro slaves suggested by the hindsight of current historians, particularly by Jewish Communist and black nationalist scholars.

Nevertheless, it was an all too easy and, as our times have shown, a shortsighted conclusion from correct observations if anyone assumed that the American Negro subculture could not conceivably clash with American values. All folk music, folk art, and folk lingo, and particularly the underground culture of the blacks, have today become the main identifying symbols, the chief *mot de parole,* of unbounded rebellion throughout our society: when they "tell it like it is" the black militants who speak in this language today fling in our faces a bitter hostility against the white majority that always pervaded what was once a hidden, private Negro culture.

Moreover, one does not need the current revisionist Negro historians to establish that the slaves were alive to the political currents affecting them, to the West Indian slave rebellions and black republics, the Nat Turners and John Browns, and the underground railroad they themselves operated together with Northern abolitionists. A chronicler as nonmilitant as Booker T. Washington records in his autobiography the quick, continuous registry and transmission of such news in the talk that flowed through the plantation slave quarters.

But the slaves, detribalized, dispersed, sold up and down the country as packages of crude labor power, neither had, nor could they have, the ability to act freely or rationally on such reports. They had no organs to construct, voice, or act out a communal consensus. They did not even share a sense of historical identity that could build on the sporadic outbreaks of resistance and servile rebellion. The tribal ties were gone together with the tribal culture, and not only were they now American Christians like their masters, but by very name and identification they were, individually, their masters' men. The plantation, the slave quarters, and field work defined the only social organization they could act in, and effectively cut off all other possibilities.

Under these circumstances one could circulate tales and legends of Toussaint and Nat Turner—though John Henry was far more feasible. One could *not* build an ethnic tradition, or a movement tradition, let alone a liberation movement. To do so retrospectively today does not endow the plantation slaves with the notion, inconceivable for them, of an independent history of their own, not to speak of an actively, freely, rationally created history.

What Jews have always had, and find it impossible to lose, is their own history. But the aching paradox of their life in the Diaspora is that they were so little able to create it fully, actively, and rationally.

The core concept that embodies and integrates the whole Jewish experience in the Diaspora is the idea of Exile. For centuries Jews conceived themselves as under a ban of penance, expelled from their own land and living in expiatory subjection to the Gentiles in countries which were not their home. Their redemption, together with the redemption of all mankind, was expected only at the millennium of their suffering; and when one millennium had passed, Jews patiently and lovingly accepted a further term of bondage and oppression that might well last for another.

The consequences of this Myth—it bulks so large in world history that it needs a capital to do it justice—were intricately involved and incalculably important in the Jewish fate and destiny. In Christian countries particularly, it had almost as large a place in Gentile conceptions of universal history as among Jews. The agreement shared by Jews and Christians that Jews had a special, cardinal role in world history, that they were chosen both for the universal redemption and for universal punishment, may have been evaluated quite differently by each, but it gave Jews a special, universally significant identity, cherished by themselves and recognized by all others in countries where Jews lived.

It is well, nevertheless, to note more precisely what the relation of Jews to real history was. In theory as well as in fact, Jews had no share in the history that was being made from day to day. Their relation to world history—by which we mean, of course, world history as conceived primarily in the Christian world—was strictly eschatological. It related in the End of

83

Days, when world history would be over, and to the Revelations and Theophanies in which it essentially began. In the interim —that is, throughout the long Exile which is the whole historical experience of Diaspora Jewry—they were under a "subjugation to the powers" who made history. For themselves, they were without the will or the capacity to shape their destiny freely, actively, rationally. They relied in this matter in principle upon the will of God.

This was not merely a resigned acceptance of insuperable obstacles to freedom, though it was that too. A characteristic theme of the normative Jewish tradition was the belief that Jews stood outside of history by virtue of a special dispensation. When astrology was an accepted science, the Jews said that there was no constellation that governed their fate. The stars and spheres which controlled all temporal affairs shaped the history of each of the other peoples. They made wars on each other and won or lost through the natural balance of the celestial forces. Jews, however, stood under the special providence of God. In their long Exile, they could make neither war nor any other calculated use of natural forces to influence their fate. They could only wait in prayer and in loving acceptance of pain for the end of history when God would again show them His favor, before the whole world.

AT SEA IN HISTORY

The medieval ghetto and the plantation slave quarters cannot be regarded as satisfactory institutions from any point of view. Setting aside all moral evaluations, one cannot even approve of them as smoothly functioning, frictionless organizations.

The massacres and expulsions which repeatedly broke the continuity of life in the ghettos, pales, and juderias of pre-Emancipation Jewry demonstrate how chronically unstable these social institutions were. The whole set-up, in many cases, was theoretically a revocable privilege granted provisionally and for limited terms to Jews. Its maintenance was often regarded as a special interest of those monarchs, nobles, and prelates who protected the Jews, rather than a matter of public interest fixed in the common, collective sense of law and justice. It was an arrangement which frequently encountered the violent opposition of the public, whose sense of fitness was outraged by the toleration of the Jews.

The American slave system, to be sure, had a firmer base in the general will of Southern society. (Its incompatibility with the Constitution and the opposition of Northern abolitionists are not pertinent to this point in the discussion.) Unlike the contingent, conditional toleration of Jews, a privilege extended to the minority by the few against the majority's will, slavery represented a vested right of the dominant class and was considered basic to the whole public interest by the Southern majority. The South's peculiar institution was a "value" for which the whole body of the whites were ready to fight and die. Nor was its permanence threatened by serious opposition or resistance by the black slaves. Yet one can hardly claim that slavery was a smooth, sweetly running, frictionless, efficient model of social organization. It worked at the cost of severe tension, and involved wastage and deterioration of human energies for all who were caught up in its grinding, clanking, wheezing machinery.

Functionally effective or not, these were fixed institutions which only settled more firmly into their established structure during their period of history. Their basic outlines, the demands they made on conduct, the reciprocal expectations entailed for people living under these systems were not easily borne but, at any rate, were easily predictable and familiar. On the other hand, the dissolution of these systems, the abolition of slavery and the ghetto, produced the modern Jewish problem and the modern American race problem.

85

Disabilities and hardships originally enforced by law, dilemmas frozen rather than solved by the old institutions were not painlessly dissolved by the mere act of emancipation. Forces of aspiration and resentment, however, were set free. A succession of problems and crises, but not yet a fixed mode of behavior that can be considered historically definitive, characterize the period of Jewish and Negro emancipation. We are still living in the turmoil of that period.

Neither Jews nor Negroes were organized to achieve their own emancipation nor ideologically committed to the liberal revolution before it happened. It came as a surprise, an unlooked for benefaction—and a challenge. Thereafter, both adopted the principles of emancipation with utopian expectations and conviction. The post-Emancipation intellectual history of American Negroes and of Jews in Western countries is primarily concerned with the dialectics of confronting these utopias with the recalcitrant realities.

Whatever else emancipation may or may not have done, it brought Jews and Negroes into the swift stream of active history. The days of Jewish detachment and seclusion from Gentile affairs and of the Negroes' enforced incapacity for any responsible action in their own or the general interest were over. They were plunged into history, but it remained to be proven that the history could be truly their own: that they were free to create it actively and rationally for themselves.

*　　　*　　　*

A universal effect of emancipation upon the Jews was to cause them to identify, for the first time truly, with the countries where they lived. The natural bonds of men with the land of their birth were, of course, always effective. Even in medieval times, the landscape, language, and manners of each country were built into the culture and identity of the Jews no less than of the Gentiles who lived there. But what made universal sense of the Jew's condition and established his historic identity —the same for all Jews—were not these local temporal values and surface colorations: it was the grand Myth of the Exile that justified and explained a Jew to himself and to the whole world. As an exile, the Jew could not feel that he was truly, historically at home in any land of the Diaspora. These were basically temporary domiciles, places of penance, from which he or his remote descendants would in the time of Redemption be brought home to Zion.

Emancipation drastically altered all this and gave the Jews, at least in their own eyes, the privilege and duty of nationality in their several countries. They became Frenchmen of the Mosaic faith, Britons or Germans of the Jewish persuasion, and, of course, Americans who belonged to—though not very often in—synagogues.

They shared in all these national histories, to the confusion of their own history and identity. The Exile, that fundamental myth of the millennial Jewish historic being in which all were united, became an ideological nuisance. It had to be denied, or transformed into a Mission, rather than a penance. Jewish Messianism, equally fundamental to the identity-culture of the people, was even more embarrassing. Its eschatological character was now abstracted from history in a manner grossly discordant to the style of traditional Jewish culture. The Messianic era became a liberal Deist utopia. Or, the Redemption was pinned down to the national history of France or America, and Paris or Baltimore was crowned with the high name of Zion. The bond of unity between all Jews in their own culture was broken. The synagogue, especially in America, was bleached to a pale Protestant neutrality, without concern on the part of radical Reformers for the fact that it then became unrecognizable as Jewish to other Jews.

That Jews threw themselves with enthusiasm into the duties

87

and privileges of citizenship goes without saying. Their talent for patriotism was remarked at once by all who studied impartially the American or French Revolutions, not to say the liberation wars of Germany, Poland, Italy, and any other country where the prospect of emancipation existed. If they were at all restrained in this ardent participation, it was not because they willingly held anything back, but because of Gentile suggestions or open complaints that the damn Jews were making themselves too much at home in national affairs.

The entry into history confronted the Jews with the modern Jewish Problem. Their own time-honored, universal identity, maintained over centuries and across seas and continents, was seriously impaired. On the other hand, hostile Gentiles now denied them full title to the new identities they severally claimed when they declared their home in Exile to be their fatherland.

Jews regarded this recalcitrance as an anachronistic survival of anti-Semitism, a relic of the benighted past. They responded by making a utopia out of Emancipation. The Jewish Problem —which, in the final analysis, meant the constraint of an unwanted Jewish identity—would be resolved when free countries were true to their own principles.

There were also conditions which had to be achieved on the Jewish side; but even before their emancipation the Jews were evidently moving in the right direction. This gave liberal Jews in their time confidence that history might favor the utopia of true Emancipation. If the old, sacral segregation of the Jews were to be overcome without their conversion, a new secular culture neutral to both Judaism and Christianity was needed as the foundation for a society open to Jews and Christians indiscriminately. In order to participate in such a culture, Jewish intellectuals would have to detach themselves from rabbinic traditions as Gentile humanists had freed themselves from theology. In order to participate in an open society, Jews of the rank and file would have to break up the tight discipline of their own communal autonomy.

Both these conditions were already well advanced in their development long before the full enfranchisement and emancipation of Jews in a democratic state was thought of, and without relation to such liberal ideals. A class of Jewish intellectuals more or less detached from rabbinic tradition became increasingly apparent in a number of Jewish communities well in the seventeenth and eighteenth centuries. Monarchs as far removed from democratic ideas as Louis XIV or Frederick the Great, Maria Theresa or Catherine of Russia were inclined to liquidate closed corporations of all kinds, including the autonomous Jewish communal organization, in order to promote their mercantilist plans for a centrally regulated society and political economy.

Before the liberal revolutions offered citizenship as a way to enter the secular national community, there were other neutral social formations in which Jews might participate as well as Gentiles. The qualifications were wealth or non-traditional culture. A rich Jewish entrepreneur in seventeenth- or eighteenth-century Amsterdam, London, or Bordeaux could participate relatively freely in the early capitalist commercial and financial society of those towns where religiously based guild restrictions did not apply. The avant-garde literary salons of Berlin and Vienna and Masonic orders in England, France, and America were open to acceptable Jews: that is, to such Jews as were visibly detached from their rabbinic superstitions and outlandish traditional customs.

Wherever agnostic science and humanistic philosophy gained a foothold or early capitalism breached the feudal frame, there were also social formations organized on secular principles. Their effect on pre-Emancipation Jewries was to divide them into categories: some, the wealthy and cultured Jews, gained

89

access to a neutral social milieu, where their religion was irrelevant; the bulk remained secluded in their religious segregation. In Russia a formal, legal "assortment" of the Jews on this basis was undertaken, and throughout the nineteenth century they remained divided between the mass confined to the Pale of Settlement and the privileged Jews admitted into inner Russia. The relationship between the few and the mass in such cases was necessarily strained and their solidarity sometimes impaired.

With the Emancipation, and particularly with the separation of church and state, notably in America, one might think that all Jews could now, in principle, seek admission into a society that was religiously neutral. This was, of course, far from true. In some countries, particularly in France and Germany, the emancipation of the Jews, together with the whole Revolution of which it was a major symbolic expression, was fiercely contested by the counterrevolutionary Right. Anti-Semitism on the Continent was as significantly politically as race bigotry in America. But even where the Jewish problem remained a minor issue, as in England or America, the emancipation opened up only restricted avenues for neutral association of Jews and Gentiles in the same community. As we have remarked earlier, not citizenship, but the church—at least, the minimum shared basis of Christian belief—was the qualifying criterion for many social, cultural, and even economic relationships.

This left two options open to the cultured or wealthy or religiously detached, but unconverted, Jew. There could be the same kind of assortative separation as was legally provided in Czarist Russia. An agnostic, nontraditional, or antitraditional Jew might virtually end his contacts with the close Jewish community and live within the available pockets of social relationship which were really neutral religiously: in the academy, or the intellectual community, or the literary-political Left. Another option was to live by, and work for, the utopia of a truly liberal, religiously neutral America of the future.

*   *   *

With emancipation, Negroes too entered, or were flung, into history. For the first time they were given the responsibility, and the opportunity, of acting on their own behalf. They were cast loose as individuals to provide for themselves and, for the first time suddenly, as a community to solve their unique common problems. Citizenship and the franchise, the individual rights of each qualified adult, at once raised the question of the capacity and qualifications of the Negro group. They were to vote, but then they must learn to read and write and arrive at independent, rational decisions. As free men they were to work and support themselves, no longer depending on their masters' care: but then they must learn new trades and how to manage their affairs.

These were tasks which required common thought and action. They had to decide whether they should concentrate their effort on the political struggle for the realization of their rights or the economic struggle for training in crafts, trades, and business; whether to build schools for the "talented tenth" who would be their leaders and teachers or concentrate on practical, industrial education for a broader mass. For all of this, they had to become a community with the essential minimum capacity to act independently, or in cooperation with groups of white philanthropists and benefactors.

Communal action required a consensus, however loose and partial; and this, in turn, required the minimal cooperation of an intellectual class. Emancipation in America not only opened new doors for educating Negro intellectuals. It gave the black teachers, writers, and professionals, whether newly trained or

91

already existing among pre-Civil War Negro freedmen, a community, however rudimentarily organized, within which to work.

Moreover, under American conditions, the undifferentiated black community, and only that community, was the sole society in which a Negro intellectual could define his identity and pursue his proper functions. There were no social formations neutral to black and white. There was not even a recognized division of strata, like the West Indian black-mulatto-white classification, which could assort and divide the Negroes, allowing the intellectual some scope to detach himself. The fact that uplift organizations working among Negroes were often white-initiated and white-directed offered black professionals or voluntary workers participating in them no opening into a color-blind society. There was only the harsh alternative, for one with a sufficiently white skin and appearance, of "passing": of living in lifelong disguise as a white man.

The intellectual was, thus, bound by fate to the community. He could harbor no utopia which viewed an available solution for his immediate problem of integration as a possible ultimate solution for other classes of Negroes as they rose to his level. Any solution would have to be, in principle, a solution for all alike, and probably for all at once.

Utopian hopes were one of many factors that helped splinter the once firmly united Jewish community. For the freed blacks, their emancipation by the whites merely posed the problem of organizing a community of the disorganized and disoriented onetime plantation slaves. The utopia of a new black emancipation, that passion between hope and despair, was a force that drove them to organize on separatist, ethnic lines.

IV. The Liberal Response

NOTHING so clearly marks the sea-change in American assumptions about domestic public affairs as the open recognition
and frank discussion of ethnic politics today. The polite fiction
that America has no minorities is completely discarded. With it
has gone the taboo that once invested the notion of ethnic and
racial politics with such pious horror.

One remembers how recent has been this change with a sense
of shock. To the end of the Sixties, we had a stable electoral
majority based on a coalition built by F.D.R. in the early Thirties. It was plainly constructed on ethnic lines, combining the
forces of Irish big city politicos and Southern courthouse politicians, and the votes of rural poor whites with those of urban
Catholics, Jews, and Negroes. This was mentioned in respectable
circles only to deplore the fact. At the same time, many of our
major policies, both foreign and domestic, expressed in reality
the ethnic predilections and prejudices of a minority of white
Anglo-Saxon Protestants, concentrated in politically overrepre-
sented farm areas and the upper strata of our society, economy,
and institutions of culture. This fact was overlooked in blank
innocence: it was considered so natural as not even to be noticed.

Today we stress ethnic factors in politics with such fiercely
partisan vehemence that much more than justice is done to the
facts. On one side "WASP" has become an explicit term of
abuse, while "black power" or the ethnic slogans of "Third
World" peoples in America—Puerto-Ricans, Mexican Americans, American Indians—command a rapt and respectful
attention. On the other side, middle America rallies its own

ethnic cohorts to elect Nixon, in a contest where backlash votes were shared by Wallace; and the prominent participation of Jewish New Left students and professors together with black militants in disruptive political demonstrations is meaningfully and ominously taken note of.

The candor of the present style has made dangerous topics commonplace and turned them into our clichés. What everybody knows and heedlessly says today was mentioned in Old America chiefly by bigots.

Bigots more truly perceived, and prejudice more significantly determined, the real situation of Jews and Negroes than well-bred liberals could then openly acknowledge. The Jew-haters felt in American Judaism, however acculturated, the lurking menace of dissent. The Negrophobes sensed among the Negroes the constant threat of disobedience. The same hatred and fear, which in bigots was an impulse to action, were widely current in more passive, contemptuous stereotypes that defined and justified the minorities' position. The Jews were contemptible cowards, but also dangerously, insidiously, malevolently cunning. The blacks might be childlike and simple, but they were dangerously primitive. Men like these were necessarily and justifiably kept out or kept down.

Stereotypes of this sort, openly voiced on any occasion by the yahoos, were conventionally covered by educated, civilized people—at least, in public or in mixed society—with a formal show of tolerance to Jews and benign good will to Negroes. The inferior social status of the minorities is more fittingly acknowledged with condescension than with contempt by a majority when it is secure. To sound an alarm of impending peril betrays insecurity in the majority.

The intuitions of prejudice were nonetheless correct in important respects. Whoever tolerates an ideological minority does harbor a carrier of dissent. The germ may lie dormant, or become encapsulated, but it constantly threatens subversion. Whoever maintains a whole race in slavery or other forms of suppression must reckon with festering resentment and possible servile rebellions, jacqueries, uprisings of the oppressed. No one considering the scene today can avoid noting the impressively large share of Jews in American dissent and of blacks in American disobedience.

The perceptions of the prejudiced may have been more correct than those of the liberals, or their formulations franker, but the practical expression of their attitudes was a paranoid extremism. Even as lunatic fringe phenomena, anti-Semitic agitators are an embarrassing heritage from the outlived past for a secular society constitutionally committed to liberal principles. White vigilantes and lynch mobs threaten the security of any orderly life. Reasonable men, let alone liberals, necessarily abhor both anti-Semitic and Negrophobic extremism.

Dissent and disobedience are now more than potentialities inherent in the minorities' situation; they pervade the whole society, with particular intensity among young Jews and blacks. The liberals of the majority must now face this problem squarely, not with veiled prejudice but in the open light of a liberal morality. Paranoid anti-Semitic and anti-Negro activities based on fear of subversion and rebellion can no longer be condemned merely on prudential grounds, as a law and order issue. The hard perceptions underlying them must be responded to with realism, as well as sanity.

And, indeed, the current liberal response *is* a moral confrontation of the grounds for dissent and disobedience among some minorities. Their restricted, segregated position, it argues, was imposed upon them by the majority rather than freely chosen by the minority. (It bears repeating again that, in the case of Jews, this is a partial truth; and indeed, Jewish dissent is not approached in the same way as Negro disobedience. But, put in relative terms, the statement holds that the contemporary American Jewish situation is more imposed than chosen.) In

95

an unbalanced relationship like this, the moral responsibility for a measured response to unrest, for keeping a balance, is greater, according to liberal lights, for those who have the upper hand. It would invert the moral scale of liberal values, and, for that matter, be neither Christian nor American, if the dominant WASPs were to yield to phobic hatred because the minorities say they hate them.

The effect of these views is to produce indulgence towards extravagant, extremist, and even paranoid acts and expressions on the part of the hard-pressed minorities. One has to understand their situation, it is said.

But there is something else implied here as well. There is a confidence that the radical militancy of the aroused minorities is, in the final analysis, fundamentally attuned to the American Way. In taking this position, apparently one concedes at the outset that the dominant WASPs may no longer exercise their privilege to determine the universal American values. One also wagers that the now uproarious minorities do not intend basic destruction, but, truly considered, want to build on the authentic American tradition, though freshly, originally, and creatively interpreted.

Like all wagers, this one, too, is a risk, not a certainty. The rhetoric of many radicals and the practices of a few could cast doubt on the assumptions underlying it. But, here again, as a relative proposition the position is more probably justified than not.

The tags and slogans of current far-out radicalism are subject to the same reservations as the stereotyped viciousness of bigots. They indicate correctly underlying facts and feelings among those they profess to speak for. Still, dissent and disobedience among minorities do not foreshadow a possible consensus that rejects but one that seeks America. Whoever truly speaks for Jews and Negroes today, among the many who claim to do so, voices an ultimate commitment to freedom in the American style. Such men are essentially liberal utopians, and the princi-

96

ples of emancipation, extended by each to the utopian limit he chooses, continue to guide them.

*   *   *

One kind of ethnic politics that used to be viewed with a certain indulgence in Old America was the mishmash of activity that went on among Jews. The public, not to speak of the politicians, fully understood, in spite of loud Jewish disclaimers, that there was a Jewish vote; but the Jews self-consciously rejected any rule of blatant ethnic selectivity and voted rather consistently for high-minded, altruistic, emphatically liberal-progressive causes. The journals reflecting Jewish opinion expressed a variety of liberal to left positions, but were known for their intellectual quality, never less than literate and often excessively highbrow. Jewish lobbies too, from the American Jewish Committee or Anti-Defamation League to the Zionist movement, won a certain repute, not to say notoriety; but the domestic measures Jews supported in their own interest were equally clearly and emphatically promoted in the interest of all those oppressed and discriminated against.

Jewish pressure on foreign policy issues aroused sharper opposition, since this seemed to imply imposing risks on others where only Jews were menaced. Jews had to work hard to persuade Gentiles that what threatened Jews would eventually threaten them too. This line of argument had much success on the left when it was voiced in the language and style of the avant-garde in the Thirties; and the course of events in Hitler Germany bore conviction to the liberal majority too. But steadily increased involvement in the war in Europe, polarizing American opinion, also heightened the intensity and tightened the political organization of right wing isolationism, including a strong component of anti-Semitism. The war was labeled a Jewish war and hatred of the Jews as warmongers rose to a peak precisely as we approached D-Day.

97

Victory and revelations of the true nature of the Nazi "final solution," the genocide in which over a third of all the world's Jews—and nearly all those in Hitler's grasp—were coldbloodedly slaughtered, altered the entire structure of Jewish ethnic politics. Political anti-Semitism, in a way worth considering more specifically, came under a general taboo in the post-Hitler world. On the other hand, Jewish activism in self-defense began to seem not only natural but ethically essential in the light of the Holocaust. Among left and liberal circles it became the mode, in due time, to castigate the Jewish victims for being inadequately activist when their own lives or self-respect were at stake.

The current line is to hurl the tag of "Jewish liberal" as a challenge at the Jewish citizen, voter, or intellectual. One is asked: How does the liberal Jew stand on the urban crisis—that is, on black nationalism; on the Middle East—that is, on Arab refugees, Palestinians, and other aspects of the Arab-Israeli conflict; or on the cold war—that is, on Vietnam and the Middle East or, on the other hand, the oppressive measures applied by the Communist apparatus against Jews in the Soviet Union and the satellite countries?

It is taken for granted in all this that Jews have a specific position and that it is liberal; for Jews are somehow political liberals by their very nature. There is a great deal of modern and contemporary evidence for such a view. After every major American election in past decades, commentators carefully examined the results for signs that Jews were finally beginning to vote like others in the same income brackets as themselves. The findings have been consistently negative. Even though there were more and more Jews in the middle classes and fewer Jewish workers or impoverished slumdwellers, they continued disproportionately to support politicians who appealed to the underprivileged, unskilled, and disaffected.

The 1968 presidential election, it was thought, should certainly bring out at last a Jewish response more appropriate to social and economic self-interest. The campaign came on the heels of a season of black unrest, one of whose major targets had been precisely the Jewish lower-middle-class elements in immediate contact with the Negro "ghetto." A Jewish backlash was expected, and with it, perhaps, a final breakthrough of Jews into more "natural" political attitudes. But once again the Jewish vote departed from normal and Jews continued disproportionately to support the same candidates who were, more appropriately, favored by Negroes and the other urban poor.

Some explanation other than the usual social and economic determinants of political behavior obviously has to be sought for this phenomenon. Lawrence Fuchs is one of many current students of the subject who readily find it in the Jewish cultural heritage: that is, in the special deposit of values supposedly left by Jewish religious tradition in the "attitudes" and "behavior patterns" of even the no-longer-observant and no-longer-believing Jews. It appears that to be Jewish means to share to some irreducible degree in a residual culture that is inherently and inescapably liberal.

*　　*　　*

To speak of "the Jew" is to speak of a long history; and whatever Jewish values may inherently and inescapably be, we could not possibly know it without taking into account a substantial part at least of the centuries of events implied in any statement about Jewish culture or tradition. Even in the foreshortened perspective of today's middlebrow intellectual conventions, it is accepted that the relevant background of Jewish liberalism goes back beyond one's parents or grandparents to the East European *shtetl* of *their* forebears. For a reasonably reliable attribution of current political behavior to Jewish tradition, one would have to draw on a much longer history and wider geography.

Not only the *shtetl* experience, up to times some of us still

99

remember, but the whole history of European Jews from Roman times to the nineteenth century argues overwhelmingly against the assumption that the Jewish tradition is inherently favorable to political liberalism. Since Hitler, no one can doubt how precarious the Jewish condition ultimately remains. Extreme "solutions" of the perennial problem of the Jews are far from being a chance aberration in history. Massacres and expulsions dot the entire record of the Diaspora and, in Europe, more densely as we go back towards the Crusades.

The common element that marks such explosions of endemic Jew-hatred into violent forms is their connection with periods of social and political upheaval in Gentile society. What safety Jews enjoyed in the long Exile depended on the maintenance of political and social stability. Rebellious Ukrainian Cossacks or German peasants killed Jews; kings and bishops did not love them, but often protected them, and if they drove them out it was usually under pressure from below.

Jews depended for their lives on the authorities, on those who exercised legitimate authority, and they were endangered whenever legitimacy broke down. This is the basic historical condition most profoundly related to the authentically Jewish, traditional political attitude. Thus, the natural Jewish political attitude, the attitude that truly expresses a continuous tradition up to and including the *shtetl,* is one of conservatism.

To an equally important degree, it was fundamentally an attitude of detachment. The root-idea and root-experience of any Jewish political tradition that may exist is the millennial Exile of the Jewish people. A people that prayed continually, on every possible occasion, to be reunited "next year in Jerusalem" did not regard any country it lived in as more than a temporary domicile. How much fervor and conviction attended this prayer certainly varied, but never until modern times need it be recited as a mere mechanical performance, let alone with the embarrassment it arouses among some contemporary Jews.

100

That Zion was his true home may not have been a profound personal experience for every Jew; but that Diaspora countries, in basic essentials, were not their true homes was an elementary fact of life for all Jews before the Emancipation. The laws and attitudes of the Gentiles around left no doubt on that score.

The most natural and, for that matter, the safest Jewish response was to steer clear of *goyish* politics. Like history, politics was a Gentile game. Jews resorted to it at their peril; and they did so, as Jews, mainly in defense of the community against specific attacks. (The Sephardi Jews, caught in the border wars of the Iberian Christians and Moors, had a somewhat different history in this respect, which goes to explain their variant Jewish cultural tradition.) If the most desirable attitude, that of total detachment, was not possible, as was frequently the case, then the ruling consideration was the fact that Jews depended on protection by the authorities for their safety. The instinct and folk wisdom of the Jews taught them to serve their masters' interests and pray for their well-being.

An Adopted Tradition

The "tradition" of Jewish liberalism is a recent development, whose relation to truly traditional Jewish values is highly questionable. It is also a very partial tradition, particularly characteristic of Western European Jews and their descendants, who are a minority among Jews. If it existed at all among Jews in Muslim countries, it only arose in exceptional cases and in near-contemporary times. Several generations ago, radical attitudes became prevalent among rebellious Eastern European Jews. While such radicalism is often called "liberal" in America, this is quite a different political stance from the true liberalism cultivated by French, British, and German Jews. American Jews inherited a composite tradition, more Eastern than Western European, which they adapted to our local conditions.

The classic home of Jewish liberalism is Western Europe; and Western Europe, for Jews, means that block of countries from the Atlantic to the line of Danzig-Prague-Vienna-Trieste where Jews were effectively emancipated in the course of the nineteenth century. Jewish liberalism originated as an afterthought of the Western Jewries faced with the French Revolution and expecting other acts of enfranchisement.

Where it was adopted, it was the hallmark of the entire community; a fact which should give us pause. Jewish liberalism was a very conventional or, as it was called in those days, a philistine political attitude. For one thing, accepting their country as their home made enthusiastic patriots of the Jews. The nation, not the lord or dynast, became the authority to whom they were bound for their protection, and their new allegiance was immeasurably deeper and more personal than the old. Whatever else a good Jew might be in post-Emancipation Western countries, he was almost always a chauvinist. No one was more loyally German than a German of the Mosaic persuasion, more ardently French than a French Israelite, or more jingoist than a Hebrew Briton.

If their patriotism was stressed, there was a good reason for it. Among Gentile patrioteers, the capacity of the Jew to belong to the nation was strenuously denied. True Gallic nationalism, of which *they* were the real judges and certified exemplars, *echtdeutschnationalismus,* or even being a true Englishman and not merely a British subject, remained forever beyond the reach of Jews. This condition required not merely the unreserved devotion Jews were prepared to offer but also acceptance by Gentiles qualified to extend acceptance. The only way to gain this natural goal of Jewish liberalism—to be the peer and fellow of all one's countrymen—was to renounce both liberalism and Judaism. To be a real German, Englishman, or Gallic Frenchman one had to convert— and adopt a position on the far political right. Even Disraeli was hardly Christian and Tory enough.

102

Against this attitude the Jewish community as a whole had to rely on a liberal definition of nationality. Only if nationality were detached from both religion and ethnic background and based solely on citizenship could a Jew really belong. The forced and defensive tone of collective liberalism in Western Jewish communities arose from the imperative necessity to adopt this position in apologetics, explicit or implied. The vociferous Jewish patriotism, demonstrated in act no less than word, was equally necessary for their public defense.

If any newly or nearly emancipated Jew in a Western country rejected the overstrained nationalism of his countrymen, both Gentile and Jewish, it was not in the name of a distinct Jewish nationalism but in the cause of leftist, especially proletarian, internationalism. Such deviants, from Ludwig Boerne to Rosa Luxemburg, were not included in the Western European Jewish consensus, since they rarely showed any interest in the Jewish community and lived outside it, or in the remotest connection. Others might think of them as Jews, especially when hostile, but they did not. Their leftist comrades were usually tactful enough to ignore the matter.

Thus, if modern Western Jews were liberal, it was partly because Jewish nonliberals, to the right and left alike, opted out of the community. A process of selection reinforced the uniform liberalism of Western Jews, and the community not only relied collectively on a liberal defense of its status but was increasingly made up of individual liberals.

As so much of the Jewish liberal doctrine was pretense, not reality, attaching itself to forms and appearances, not substance, it had a peculiarly hollow quality. It was a commitment of a kind that could be shared by all who remained within the community, no matter how far apart they stood on such significant issues as religious belief.

Religious liberal reformers might feel uneasy about the tradition that they were in Exile and consequently eliminated prayers for Messianic redemption in Zion from their liturgy.

Orthodox Jews, standing stiffly on the whole tradition, could just as truly affirm their total commitment to the nation-states of France, Germany, England, or America. Their vigorous patriotism was undiminished by their eschatological beliefs, which referred to Kingdom Come, not any mundane political allegiance. Attachment to one's fatherland was also expressed in the Western Jew's full acculturation to its national language, manners, and prejudices. This, too, was shared by all, from the farthest right to the farthest left in religious orientation.

The liberal commitment to one's country validated religious differences as a private concern. Common adherence to this principle was the base and substance of a liberalism shared by the whole Western Jewish community. There was not too much else to it; and intellectuals who abandoned the community on the left and the right drew blood when they scoffed at the philistinism of the Jewish liberal bourgeoisie.

* * *

It follows that Jewish liberalism was a notably self-regarding ideology, though there was nothing it was less willing to face than this fact. Its root and primary principle was the wishful thought that after their emancipation Jews were the same as Gentiles in everything outside the synagogue. This meant, of course, that Gentiles were expected to drop all exclusions and discriminations against Jews—which signifies all preferences for Christians—not only in state offices and public institutions, but in everything short of the church. The demand was silly, or at best naïve: the church ties in with the family and with intimate circles of neighborliness and friendship in a wide net of natural preferences and elective affinities that cannot be abolished at the drop of a political pronouncement.

Belief in a doctrinaire, simplistic liberalism that ignored these facts could not seem the same in a Jew as in a Christian. As Jews had everything to gain, radically consistent liberalism on their part looked like manipulation, deliberate or not. A Christian, who had everything to lose, looked magnanimous, or else weakly foolish, when he was willing to yield to the moral blackmail of Jewish liberalism.

The fantasy of a neutral society for Jews and Christians apart from religion did not materialize, of course, in any country. In Western Europe, on the Continent, liberal secularism provoked a fierce and public resistance. Counterrevolutionary forces in France and Germany, upholding the traditions of the *ancien régime* and the idea of the Christian state, fought the equal admission of Jews, or other dissenters, to public office and even to citizenship as a major issue in national politics. The Jewish question, which ultimately helped deliver Germany and virtually the whole of Europe into the hands of Hitler, significantly divided the Continental nations all through the nineteenth and to the middle of the twentieth century.

The identification of liberals as friends of the Jews and reactionaries as their enemies could hardly be avoided when, as on the Continent, the emancipation of the Jews continued to be a salient political issue. Anti-Semitism as a favorite slogan of the counterrevolution meant that Jews had to be liberal. The very basis upon which the whole community adjusted to the end of the ghetto required that the liberals win, or their gains be preserved. Not only did some Jews become prominent in liberal politics, militants in the revolutions of 1830 and 1848 and activists in the liberal parties of their countries; the whole community understood that its status depended on the maintenance of certain basic liberal principles.

But Jews, as Jews, had no idea of burning anything down in the cause of the common Jewish liberalism. (Individuals detached from the community were radical enough for anyone.) The problems ordinary Jews faced after emancipation were not primarily political. Even where the Jewish question was recurrently prominent as a national issue, the day-to-day problems of Jews had to do with social and, above all, economic

105

adjustment to the gap between doctrinaire liberal expectations and their actual situation. The Jewish question was not discernible as a clear issue between liberals and conservatives in countries like England or America. Tories, not Whigs, took the conclusive steps in what might be called Jewish emancipation in England; and in America the nearest approaches to political anti-Semitism up to World War I were made by left-leaning nativist groups, abolitionists, or populists, and not by establishment conservatives. Yet nowhere did the social and economic adjustment of Jews encounter more effective illiberal social restrictions than in English-speaking countries. Hitler refugees in New York in the late Thirties and the Forties would frequently express astonishment at barriers to contacts with Gentile America that they had never encountered in Weimar Germany.

Jewish immigrants in New York and London lived in what were miscalled by Louis Wirth "ghettos": segregated slums maintained not by law but by social conditions. Gentiles restricted their residential quarters against Jews and Jews swarmed together for mutual support and comfort. Jews flocked to the same occupations, beginning with sweatshop labor in dominantly Jewish industries and spreading out into commerce and the professions. The special occupations which continued to characterize Jews even in their rapid spread and rise from the original narrow economic base were chosen on fairly obvious principles, which had nothing whatever to do with liberalism. They were determined by their kinship to old Jewish skills and by the ruling criterion of availability. As the safe, lucrative, already established openings were filled by the recognized, if tacit, ethnic preferences of the dominant majority, Jews went into high risk areas where each man made his own way. They became salesmen, taxi drivers, dentists, opened their own law offices, wrote if they could not get teaching sinecures, and went into pioneer industries like the movies, television, plastics, or electronics.

106

Jews did not fail to fight discrimination, in housing, education, employment, public accommodations, in the name of liberalism. But their own highly successful social and economic adjustment was not won by storming the breastworks of entrenched illiberalism. They skirted these barriers—that is, they avoided the issue and went on ahead.

It is therefore a very partial description of the facts to say that the principle of equal opportunity and advancement by merit became a specifically Jewish liberal principle, identified with out of interest by the immigrants. In the fields open to them, they advanced, to be sure, by applying this principle. They supported it when it rose as an issue in general society. But where equal opportunity was denied by the general society, the Jews overcame their difficulties not collectively by a political attack on privilege but individually by seeking opportunities not already allocated to the privileged.

The circumstances in which Jewish liberalism arose did not favor their collective political activity. The politics of ethnic power depend on attitudes of group solidarity and self-assertion which were discouraged by the demands of a doctrinaire liberalism regarding the adjustment of the Jewish community to freedom. Emancipation and Western enlightenment required breaking down the tight communal discipline and cultural isolation of the traditional ghetto. This prerequisite, already well advanced in Western countries in the eighteenth century before true Emancipation was seriously contemplated, was explicitly defined by the intellectual world and peremptorily imposed by modern-minded rulers. After the Revolution granted Jews full or partial citizenship together with civil rights, and liberalism became the established position of the community, the mood of young, advanced Western Jews favored still further loosening the communal structure and reducing the singularity of Jewish customs.

Different conditions produced different results in the move-

107

ment for religious reform that arose in Western Jewish communities. In America it led to a division of the Jews into three denominations and a communal organization able only with difficulty to give some central direction to local synagogues, charities, and membership societies voluntarily incorporated, voluntarily joined, and conducted by a voluntary consensus and leadership. Governmental control in Continental countries did not permit such fragmentation, but the discipline of the Jewish community was sharply reduced by eliminating traditional functions that exceeded the limits of religion as defined in Western European secular and, especially, liberal states.

Jews tried to maintain liberalistic restrictions on the scope of religious association with more consistency than their Gentile neighbors. Catholics in France, Germany, and Italy never hesitated to organize sectarian political parties. Western Jews abhorred the idea of a Jewish vote, let alone a Jewish party; and only in desperation at the line taken by German liberal parties did some liberal Jews at the turn of the century briefly consider following the Catholic example. The same deliberate avoidance of Jewish associations in matters not directly related to worship applied beyond the sphere of politics, but here too Gentile attitudes produced difficulties and paradoxical consequences for the rigidly consistent liberalism of Jews. Germany is again the classic case: because Jews were excluded from Gentile Masonic orders and student fraternities—later, from the youth movements of German secondary school students or clerks and apprentices—they were compelled to organize their own. In such cases, the new lodges or fraternities were often declared to be "nonsectarian," and conducted in that manner, though composed almost entirely of Jews, with sometimes a token representation of Gentiles.

The Jewish liberal who could not achieve a truly neutral society for everyone made his own segregated Jewish society look as neutral as possible, while waiting for the Gentile world to catch up. But the implied reproach that only Gentile inconsistency and lack of liberal principles kept the Jews apart may be doubted even in the case of the all-Jewish "nonsectarian" Masonic orders or country clubs. One is entitled to suspect that the most liberal of Jews often felt more comfortable together and preferred each other's company to that of liberal Gentiles. There still remained too many points at which Jews and Gentiles had to be careful or silent for fear of injured sensitivities to permit their easy intimacy in common associations.

To be truly freed from the conflict of backgrounds in a neutral association meant to accept fully a consensus position regarding *every* difference of inbred responses and values; and considering the proportions of Jews to Christians in all Western societies, it is obvious how the consensus would be weighted. A wide acceptance of Christian symbolisms—from Christmas trees, Gentile given names and surnames, Easter eggs, and Sunday Sabbaths to outright Jewish self-hatred—was generally prevalent among Western Jews, but it was not enough. If the professedly neutral association was not to become a Jewish nonsectarian body, as for example the New York Ethical Culture Society, the thorough absorption of anti-Semitic attitudes and expressions, to a degree possible only for one who has turned his back consciously and completely on the Jews, was necessary.

The vulgarity of Karl Marx's references to Jews in his correspondence with Friedrich Engels testify to a Gentile anti-Semitism so thoroughly absorbed as to have become quite neutral, scarcely expressing any longer the feeling of self-hatred. Many Jewish leftists in Western countries testified by a similar freedom and naturalness in their anti-Semitic attitudes that their Jewish feelings had been almost completely obliterated. The key to this adjustment was the equal freedom to be anti-Semitic acknowledged as the right of Gentile leftists since they too (nominally at least, if not as truly as their Jewish comrades) had rejected their own past. One can readily understand why mutual acceptance of such conditions was not quite as possible for Jewish and Gentile liberals.

That liberalism involved pretense and inhibited frankness is evident not only in the strange phenomenon of Jewish non-sectarianism but in major organizations Jews created for their expressly sectarian interests. I do not refer here to the German Jewish league against anti-Semitism, which was made up of Jews and Gentiles in about the same way that the American NAACP had mixed black and white leadership and supporters. I have in mind the Alliance Israelite Universelle and similar Jewish agencies, organized for the defense of coreligionists just as the Alliance Protestante Universelle was expressly organized to defend Protestant interests. The actual nature of the work done—political intercession, aid to emigrants, vocational re-training, colonization—did not fall short of the scope of activi-ties later undertaken by secular Zionists as an open program of ethnic politics. But in rationalizing its work, the Alliance al-ways described it, with emphasis, as strictly limited to philan-thropic assistance for fellow members of the Jewish faith.

Most agencies of this kind, to be sure, were concerned with the hardships of the unemancipated Jews of Eastern Europe, North Africa, and the Ottoman Empire. The problems there were such that activities strictly confined to the sphere liberalism conceded to religion—that is, the organization of worship and other recognized acts of piety—would have been totally ir-relevant.

NEW WORLD LIBERALS

Eastern Europe is the background from which came the immedi-ate forebears of the bulk of contemporary American Jews. In comparison with the preponderant Eastern European influence, German Jewish attitudes, although built into the Jewish com-munal establishment which the great immigration found here

110

upon arrival, had a relatively minor impact on current political positions.

The special quality of politics in Eastern European Jewry derives from the fact that liberalism of the Western type was never a viable alternative for them. There was no occasion in the nineteenth-century history of Russia, Rumania, or Galicia, the Polish province of Austria, when equal rights were presented as a real possibility for all Jews in those countries. At most a thin stratum of Jews especially qualified, according to Gentile standards, were offered professional and personal advantages at the price of identification with an officially anti-Jewish regime. The legal "assortment" of Jews in Russia selected a small section for admission into inner-Russian lands and the liberal fringe of society while the bulk of Russian Jewry were formally declared "useless" and confined to the shrinking Pale of Settlement. In Galicia, some select Jewish types were admitted into the Polish national parliamentary bloc, as makeweights in the multinational Austro-Hungarian political tug-of-war. But, here too, the bulk of the Jews were locked out of such fellowship with cold decisiveness.

Under the circumstances Jews adopted one of two attitudes, or a mixture of both. The traditional community, in tight though no longer legally recognized solidarity, continued to avoid contact with any *goyim* as much as possible. Young progressives (enjoying considerable understanding, if not sympathy, on the part of their elders) pinned their hopes on revolution. This involved for some, especially those who were just as broadly educated as the Jews selected for access to polite Gentile society, renouncing ethnic Jewish loyalties for the sake of political activism among Gentiles.

But, given the dense concentration of Jews living in Russia and Austria-Hungary and the high proportion of the oppressed poor and workingmen among them, the Jewish masses themselves offered a rewarding field for political action. Once ini-

111

tiated, radical agitation and propaganda among Russian Jews produced some of the earliest and most effective leftist labor organizations. The Jewish workers so organized were no less ethnically Jewish in their attitudes than the traditionalists who dominated the Eastern European inner-Jewish establishment. Even within the confines of the Bund, the major Jewish Social Democratic labor movement which lived in constant dread of being called nationalist, an irreducible ethnic element had to be respected, on pain of alienating members: Jewish rights were specifically defended, by a specifically Jewish socialist organization, and at least a cultural ethnicism was fostered. It need hardly be said that, in spite of sharp differences and the avoidance by some of certain specific "bourgeois" associations, the Jewish socialist workers felt and acted as part of the broad, loose Jewish community.

The same may obviously be said of another rebellious Jewish group, the Zionists, whose basic motivation was to reassert ethnic loyalties. United in their nationalistic passion, the Zionists were widely divided in their other political attitudes. Every current political view from left to right, in forms which respected the right of Jewish national existence, found expression in the Zionist movement. They were, in this respect, a paradigm of the Eastern European Jewish community generally; for, apart from their specific ideological nationalism, the Zionists fully exemplified the range of the whole community's political expression and most truly revealed the key in which it was pitched.

In two ways, then, Eastern European Jewry differed sharply from the political complexion of Jews to the West. Within the ethnically identified community—and this was the overwhelming mass—there was no exclusive commitment to liberal views, but the whole gamut of political positions from left to right was acceptable and, indeed, expressed. As in the West, positions rejecting a Jewish ethnic commitment were held by a few apostates on the far right but primarily by groups of liberals and leftists with marginal, not to say evanescent, relations to the community. Leftist Jewish cosmopolitan revolutionaries, in particular, faded in and out, but more usually out, of effective contact with the mass of Jews. But in contrast with the Western situation, it was not a reliable sign that one had abandoned the Jews if one held nonliberal political views. For every rightist or leftist (or, for that matter, liberal) Jew who opted out of the community, there were many more who remained and were primarily active within.

* * *

This parental heritage provides a background for the political attitudes of most contemporary American Jewish youth and intelligentsia, to the extent they still have Jewish roots. It is true that the conditions of American life favor a Western European philistine liberalism as the collective Jewish political attitude. Emancipation preceded the arrival of any significant number of Jews here. Under the constitutional separation of church and state, Jewish ethnic tradition is substantively ignored, and the accepted designation of the Jews as a "religion," in the WASP sense, nominally denies it. Furthermore, German Jews, fully molded in the patterns of Jewish liberalism, effectively constructed a national Jewish establishment, long dominated it exclusively, and still wield major influence. In spite of all that, American Jewry has thoroughly absorbed the pattern of Eastern Europe.

Paternalistic German Jewish control of American Jewry was cracked by Eastern European rebels at least sixty or seventy years ago. Leftist political attitudes formulated in ethnic terms were consolidated, acknowledged by the consensus as authentically Jewish expressions, and have remained continuously active in the community since before World War I. Rightist positions, represented in some sense from the beginning among

113

Orthodox Jews, have recently been intellectually fortified and emerged as a self-conscious activist element among the young, as well as the older traditionalists.

It must be well understood, of course, that America is not Eastern Europe. Neither nonliberal politics nor ethnic interests are pursued by Jews in the same uninhibited way. Leftists and rightists may fight conventional liberals within the community on essentially internal issues, such as support for Yiddish-language schools or a more democratic organization of the community, and sometimes on broader questions like the issue of public aid to parochial schools. But they rarely attempt to mobilize the community as such in support of general leftist or rightist policies for America as a whole; on these issues they work individually through the general American parties.

As for specific ethnic demands, American Jews do not organize politically in national or local Jewish parties in order to promote them; nor do they favor such programs as the Eastern European conception of publicly supported, autonomous Jewish-language schools. The nearest approaches to such ideas, Horace Kallen's "cultural pluralism" or Mordecai M. Kaplan's doctrine of an "organic community," fall far short of the explicitly political ethnicism of the Eastern European parallels; they rely essentially on voluntary association rather than public law for the proper organization of Jews, among other ethnic minorities.

The notion that Jews take no stand collectively in general politics is obviously encouraged, if not specifically sanctioned, by the anarchic disorganization and baroque elaboration of intermingled agencies and cliques, agglomerated to make up the so-called Jewish community. There is no way to be authorized to represent such a collectivity in politics. Leaders with personal prestige representing one or more powerful Jewish part-organizations feel free, however, to support essentially liberal ideas in the collective name. These are carefully chosen consensus positions which need not seriously divide the constituency but represent an acceptable middle ground for American Jews, whatever one may say of other Americans. Or, like rigid support of the secular public school, they consecrate the American constitutional principle that Jewishness, like other religions, has no standing and, nominally at least, makes no difference beyond the sphere of worship. Such devout, conventional liberalism, continually proclaimed by American Jewish leaders, unites two, rather disparate, strands in the history of Jewish political attitudes: the traditional Jewish reliance on the constituted authorities—in America, constitutionally liberal; and, in its devoted Americanism, the more recent tradition of strongly stressed patriotism.

If Jewish America is not Eastern Europe, it is certainly not Western Europe either. Whatever the collective position, in their individual attitudes American Jews significantly reflect their Eastern European origins. (Even the influential German intellectual immigration produced by Hitler represents a generation of whom many had essentially Eastern European parentage and others identified vicariously with Eastern European Jewry.) A conformist liberalism is not a position precisely tailored to command enthusiastic or disciplined adherence among our metropolitan Jews. Not enthusiasm but responsible commitment impels some nonliberals to fight for certain right or left positions on inner-Jewish questions, but many more carry their ardent radical enthusiasm into general American politics. This is done in blithe, unconscious disregard, or sometimes disdain, of any inhibitions which concern for the Jewish community or its interests might suggest.

Statistically summed up, and allowing for a fairly wide spread from the norm, the political responses of American Jews represent a "liberal" position in the American sense: that is, one well to the left of center of the general American response, demanding institutional change beyond what is presently established in America. This position (subject, of course, to considerable shifts in the past and, no doubt, even more in the future) is the resultant of complex factors including the fol-

115

lowing obvious ones, whose relation to Jewish tradition is certainly various.

First, after Hitler, Jews cannot easily profess extreme rightist positions: an explicit Jewish fascism, let alone Nazism, is impossible; and to be a rightist in any sense, a Jew requires, in an exceptional degree, the courage of his convictions. Secondly, leftism, including a cosmopolitanism that denies Jews the right of separate ethnicity, is, on the other hand, a quite possible political tradition for Jews. It does not involve what Jews universally, or always (but only some factions among them, and the general consensus in some circumstances) would brand as betrayal. Leftist extremism, indeed, is the most available outlet for the widespread response of Jewish self-hatred, or the milder forms of self-denigration in which this syndrome more frequently expresses itself among American Jews in our time. Thirdly, the American Jewish community is thoroughly disorganized and undisciplined in comparison with Continental Jewries; and fourthly, it is largely made up of East European Jews.

Under these circumstances, the Jewish liberalism quite regularly referred to as "philistine" in Europe was considerably gingered up in America. There were certain countervailing factors: the self-interest and suppressed but hardly dissipated, traditionally cautious conservatism of the Jewish community still operate effectively; and, on the other hand, postliberal radicals tend, though not as decisively as in Europe, to detach themselves more than others from the Jewish establishment. The resulting Jewish communal position is consequently weighed down to a more moderate slant than might otherwise obtain. Even so, it is far to the left of normal for their social and economic position.

*　　*　　*

The assumption that social and economic interests should determine votes, while rational enough, is, of course, generally inadequate to explain complex political realities. In American experience political traditions have had at least as much to do with determining why some groups vote Republican and others Democrat. But even allowing for this, it must be conceded that Jewish votes defy explanation on the usual rationalistic grounds far more seriously than others do. And one cannot rely on tradition to explain the difference; not, at least, in the sense that it does so for other Americans.

What is called a political tradition for Northern WASPs and Southern whites is not merely a set of values that motivate individuals. It is not simply that men vote as their parents and grandparents voted. Politicians and political power have a recognized place in the elite structures of groups that truly follow a political tradition. Hence, by the way, it is false to assume that votes given on traditional grounds may be arbitrarily allocated without reference to rational interests. A political tradition built on the group's recognition of politicians among its elite represents a pragmatic adjustment to social and economic interests consistent with maintaining consensus in the group.

It is striking that Jewish politicians have never had a recognized role among American Jews in any way comparable with their status in other groups. Not only the WASPs, with their established top leaders in national and local government, but the Irish, the Italians, and the Negroes, among other minority groups, accepted the ethnic politician, from ward-heeler to mayor and Congressman, as an essential instrument of their group adjustment. When one speaks of a political tradition among them, it means a habit firmly rooted in the acknowledged leadership of politicos regularly active in the interests of the group. A Jewish politician is regarded as a Jew who is taking one of many available ways, and not a very noteworthy way, to advance himself in American society. If he gains the respect and recognition of Jews for his role, it is never at the ward-heeler's level or as an ethnic politician; it is only when he attains the stature of leadership in general American affairs.

117

The Jews have never bothered to elect a Jewish mayor of New York; and LaGuardia does not represent an exception.

The habit of American Jewish voters, consequently, is to vote as independents. What this entails is that they approach political issues abstractly, like intellectuals: in broad general lines, not out of a clear attachment to specific interest. When ignorant Jews vote for the man, not the issue, the man they vote for is the big man, the broad-gauge leader, the symbol of generous, magnanimous impulses and not necessarily the close, familiar, and reliable ethnic figure. This produces a bias towards liberalism rooted precisely in the lack of a functioning ethnic political tradition.

These tendencies are reinforced by the fact that the nearest thing to a politically active ethnic machine that existed among American Jews were the Jewish trade unions. Other Jewish organizations lobbied for liberal policies which served ethnic interests, like antidiscrimination laws; and, as lobbyists, they were concerned to maintain a proper distance and neutrality towards regular partisan politics. The Jewish trade unions were always politically aware and active, and were often outspokenly partisan —but in the class interest. Ethnic concerns, to the extent they were recognized at all, were relegated to special bodies like the Jewish Labor Committee, active within the established bounds and forms of the inner-Jewish community. A general political agency created largely by the Jewish trade unions, like the Liberal Party of New York, was not only presented as nonsectarian but disdained such minor matters as Jewish ethnic concerns.

When Jews under LaGuardia or Wagner became prominently active in the civil service and practical politics of New York City, they were drawn particularly from the ranks of Jewish labor and independents. The highpoint of "Jewish" political influence was probably signalized by the phrase "clear it with Sidney," attributed to F.D.R. The Jewish labor leader, Sidney Hillman, built his power in total disregard of any Jewish ethnic

118

concerns; and he gained prestige among Jews rather than lost it, on balance, because of this fact.

All sorts of political attitudes, left or right and not merely liberal, are possible for American Jews while remaining attached to the community and even active within it. The community itself also conducts collectively, through a set of loose-coupled and often clashing agencies, political activities. These mainly take the form of lobbying, and are therefore professedly nonpartisan, no matter how left-of-center some of the causes may appear to middle America. Openly partisan politics is still, as in Western Europe, an activity that Jews, as ethnic representatives, abjure in America. The Eastern European tradition of Jewish parties engaged in general politics (which was subject to its own restrictions even there) survives in only a few, minor organizations. To become militantly active in general politics an American Jew detaches himself, if not from the Jews, at any rate from Jewish organizations. The kind of political lobbying, intercession, public relations work, and propaganda (though not the mass pressure tactics) characteristic of Jewish organizations is, by comparison, comparable to the philistine liberalism of Western European Jewries.

V. Liberal Utopianism

IT cannot be overlooked that to be a liberal in Western Europe meant, initially and inherently, to adopt a militant position. Beginning with the *ancien régime* as its base, the mildest liberal program called for radical change. The rational, secular approach of liberals implied a vigorous activism that could not live comfortably with unsolved problems. In contrast, the philistine quality of European Jewish liberalism and the establishment-status of the liberal American Jewish community entail a placid, patient, moderate infrapolitical type of behavior that is hard for an active rationalist to accept. The Jewish liberal community has a built-in generation gap: it inculcates attitudes that lead its sons to disdain or abandon it.

Jewish liberalism, which conceived itself as a radical break with the unhappy past of Exile, ended in essentially the same dilemma as traditional Jewry but with fewer cultural resources to bear it. Jews emancipated on the theory that religion was a private affair did not turn out to be the same, except for their religion, as everybody else. Those who identified religiously with Judaism found "Jew" to be an ethnic category as well, with social and economic consequences. Those who had abjured religion found that even this did not make them the same as unbelieving ex-Christians, but they continued to be treated and classed as Jews. Since neither type saw the use of ethnic political power as a suitable method to alter the invisible barriers of their segregation, they could do little but wait for time to solve their problem. In this they fell back into the traditional attitude of the Jews in Exile.

The Jews, I have noted, were an ideological group that sur-

120

vived in defeat. Their survival was due to their own ideological stubbornness—they were willing to challenge martyrdom rather than convert—and to the reasonableness of Gentiles. To put Jews to ultimate tests meant disturbing the law and order of society as a whole; and only reckless or fanatical or maniacal Jew-haters, when they came to power, thought this game was worth the candle. So Jews were tolerated—in Catholic countries, as the sole religious dissidents—while more or less elaborate myths and rationalizations were developed to justify their peculiar status.

Jews, for their part, built quite as rich a legendary, theological tradition to cultivate an appropriate response to their Exile over interminable generations. Their inherent obligation as an ideological group to overcome rival ideologies was first of all conceded to be impossible within the frame of history: the minimum condition for their toleration was often that they should not proselytize. If they were unable to prevail over the Gentiles, but could only survive by resisting, then it was up to God to redeem both the unbelievers and the Jews. The Jewish tradition was a refined culture largely concerned with teaching Jews, individually and collectively, to wait for the Messiah.

They were, one might say, the classic example of passive resistance as a way of life; except that they did not conceive this as an effective tactic for regenerating and reconciling their enemies. Their passivity reached deeper than this. Their persecutors too, indeed all of history, were mere agencies of God to achieve His inscrutable but ultimately certain end: the redemption of mankind through ethical trial from the travail of history. As God punished His chosen people with the rod of men, so in His own good time would He break their rod; and Jews least of all were called upon to do anything but bear it in loving piety.

The culture of endurance summed up in the concept of Exile was one of the chief barriers to successful emancipation that Jewish liberalism sought to overthrow. This means that the

121

liberal, confronted with his Jewishness as a problem, must become active again: active in the world, in the rational solution of such problems. When some liberal rabbis, like the American Isaac Mayer Wise, declared that the Christian world did not yet truly understand ethical monotheism and prophetic ethics, and that Reformed Judaism must convert them, they were giving an appropriate response to this need for activism.

Most liberal Jews were not interested in so bold a program as this. The most they could countenance was some quiet public relations work against anti-Semitism. They relied mainly on efforts to reform Judaism towards a rational model which they thought might also come to prevail among liberal Christians. What utopia stood at the end of this convergence was not clear; it may not have meant destroying the Jewish-Christian difference, but only making it innocuous.

Renouncing ethnic self-assertion—that is, ideological religion—and ethnic self-interest—that is, collective political action—liberal Jews leave themselves only traditional Jewish passivity to fall back on; but without the profound culture required to carry it off successfully as a way of life. For a liberal must be rational and solve problems, not accept them as mysteries.

Problems not solved in action can, of course, be solved in imagination, but only pious people can truly live with such solutions. The liberal equivalent of prophecy is prediction; and the liberal Jewish adjustment did involve a rational belief in progress through history. They diagnosed the barriers to Jewish-Gentile equality and brotherhood as a product of ignorance, and predicted that the obstacles would fall with the advance and spread of knowledge. But unlike prophecy, whose faithful will wait for millennia in glad and ardent belief, prediction must have tangible confirmation at reasonable intervals.

*   *   *

The Jewish liberal's hope was repeatedly disappointed throughout the nineteenth and twentieth centuries. It is impossible to talk about these matters today without noting the impact of our own generation's traumatic experiences. One may sometimes have to dig deep to find the traces, for only a few individuals, especially sensitive or most drastically affected, undergo radical conversion of values even after the gravest shock. But, having seen the Hitler holocaust on one hand and the founding of Israel on the other, the toughest-minded Jews of our generation must adjust to major shifts in the coordinate axes of the whole Jewish frame of reference in order to retain their former convictions.

For one thing, the conventional liberal assumptions of Western Jewries are irrevocably outdated on the point of the Jewish-Gentile relationship. No one today can give implicit confidence to the belief that, outside the church and synagogue, nothing fundamentally divides the two. The Jew who survived Hitler, though he may not understand what ideological grounds could justify his fate, is constantly aware that the ultimate penalty of ideological dissidence, in the form of genocide, is possible—for him and for his children as well as for all those who were slaughtered in his time without cause. One may dismiss this knowledge from thought, but it nevertheless determines the basic defensive attitude in which Jews today face the world—once more, after several generations of Western Jews who stood with open arms.

The liberal pose of nonsectarian openness in everything beyond the synagogue was a pretense when maintained by purportedly nonsectarian bodies with all-Jewish membership, or by organizations purportedly religious which worked for the legal and political defense and economic and social welfare of Jews everywhere. It relied on the pretension that the Jewish interests such organizations served were universal interests; that threats to such interests were aimed in essence at all men; and that the

123

support of all men of good will could reasonably be expected for demands which only incidentally, in the given case, happened to be perceived by Jews first. Today it is basic knowledge that Jews are isolated—and together. In the last resort, they will not be effectively aided by others; but in the last resort, they will help each other.

This knowledge is there despite the fact that, for some Jews, the rise of Israel provided an escape hatch from the siege mentality that bears down on all of us. Arthur Koestler stated it flatly when he said, soon after Israel arose, that he was now free to stop being a Jew, since the Jewish state defended Jewish existence. In the light of subsequent events, this could seem like a prophetic flash from the subconscious, implying the wish that Israel, like a lightning rod, might draw down the murderous impulse of anti-Semitism upon itself, diverting it from us in the Diaspora. But when something like this, indeed, proved to be the case, and Jews in the world saw Israel, isolated, about to be offered up to genocide, they did not react with nonsectarian neutrality, or with relief at not being personally involved. They reacted with Jewish solidarity.

Nevertheless, whoever was unwilling to accept Jewish ethnic separatism before Hitler or Jewish ethnic solidarity before Israel will not abandon his conscious principles, however clearly his defensive posture betrays even to himself his gut-awareness of the facts. Old-time self-hatred and conscious rejection of Jewish ties are difficult today after the recent dread experiences of isolation and the visceral response of solidarity; yet one can still fall back to secondary defenses of the same attitudes. One can entertain a kind of Jewish self-disdain and consciously belittle the contemporary significance of Jewishness, in this way preserving the Jewish liberal's utopian passivity. Or, one can turn militant and seek to overcome Jewish isolation and solidarity by actively imposing the Jewish liberal utopia upon the Gentiles.

Militant utopian liberalism was characteristic of Jews in

124

Eastern Europe, and of some Jewish religious liberals today. In either case, their militancy conflicts with their liberalism.

Eastern Europeans rebelled against the passivity of the liberal stand with a reassertion of ethnic politics. The equality they could not achieve through emancipation as individuals was now fought for in a campaign of collective autoemancipation. They were nationalists of various shades and intensities, from Zionists who sought a national liberation in the ancestral homeland to Bundists whose autonomous Jewish labor organization was justified by a rather thin program of cultural national minority rights. In any case, they construed the rights of man to include the equal rights of nationalities, a logically difficult point to be derived from the essentially individualistic doctrine of liberalism.

The postwar campaign for an ecumenicist revision of Christian doctrine designed to eliminate the religious sources of anti-Semitism is another expression of militant utopian liberalism. It represents a sharp break with the traditional Jewish attitude. It was inherent in the concept of Exile that Jews could not, and should not seek to, convert the Gentiles. No traditional Jew, however convinced of the falsity of Gospel history, would think of denying Christians the right to consider Jews the anti-Christ. They could hardly conceive how one would remain a Christian if he abjured the theological sources of anti-Semitism. To overcome it was a task for the Messiah, not for Jew or Gentile.

Rational secularists, of course, could only regard Jew-hatred as a human problem, but neither Jewish nationalists nor radical activists proposed to overcome it by direct action. Zionists were inclined to take anti-Semitism as a fact, for, as an ethical problem and a moral responsibility, it belonged to the Gentiles. But they held to a sociological doctrine that Jew-hatred was necessarily caused by Jewish homelessness and would disappear when the national home was built and the exiled Jewish masses were gathered in. So, too, Jewish radicals analyzed anti-Semitism as incidental to the class struggle and expected it to disappear in the ruins of the capitalist system.

Those who made a direct attack on anti-Semitism were Jewish liberals. Not, however, in the militant fashion of the recent demands that the Vatican Council formally renounce old formulas and traditional views concerning the Jews' role in sacred history. Liberalism is logically incompatible with demands that groups adopt or reject specific views; though it may also be psychologically incompatible with the patience to suffer social oppressions and restraints grounded in prejudice. What Jewish liberals commonly did was to rely on the anticipated spread of knowledge to eliminate prejudice, and, in the meantime, they tried to counteract anti-Semitism by standard liberal methods of argument and persuasion.

ANTI-SEMITISM AND THE FUTURE

The primary index of the state of the Jewish problem for liberals is the current prevalence and intensity of anti-Semitism. A simple view of what constitutes anti-Semitism is taken: quite naturally in the light of Hitler, it is regarded as a specific form of hostility that leads to genocide. There is a straight line of development from the common stereotypes of thoughtless Jew-hatred to political programs for the systematic expulsion or murder of Jews. And the social and economic conditions that produce Jew-hatred are conceived in equally simple terms: ignorance that permits traditional prejudices to flourish; poverty or "relative deprivation," particularly the trauma of loss of status, of "declassment," that produce the social pathologies of violence; and specifically, the salience of differences between Jews and Gentiles, which single out the Jew as a classic scapegoat.

This description and diagnosis of the disease logically leads on to prescriptions for curing it. Genocide can be prevented by eliminating prejudice, the root of hatred, and overcoming poverty and deprivation, the sources of violence. The Jewish scapegoat function could be neutralized by diminishing the dissimilarities of Jews and Gentiles, or at least the saliency of remaining differences. The clue to all these therapies lies in a connected chain of social, economic, and cultural changes: a more urbanized, upwardly mobile, economically secure, and better educated American population will necessarily be less prejudiced, violence-prone, and fixated on anti-Jewish stereotypes.

The more simplistic versions of this liberal analysis are no longer tenable in our generation. We can barely recall when the Jewish problem was construed by friends of the Jews as the question whether civil emancipation would, indeed, remove the causes of the ghetto Jew's cultural backwardness, economic noxiousness, and antisocial clannishness. Emancipated Jews reached the peaks of Western culture and economic achievement and they displayed a passion for open association on neutral grounds. Yet in each respect, the pursuit of freedom produced a Jewish distinctiveness not necessarily chosen by the Jews. Their very success in adjusting to freedom provoked the resentment of relatively deprived groups, who attached to the newly visible liberalistic signs of Jewishness—literacy, professionalism, free thought, cosmopolitan manners and associations and, above all, wealth—the stigma of their virulent traditional hatreds. Moreover, even in those circles where the Jew was tolerated, the condition for his full acceptance as brother and equal, as fellow-national or social peer, usually remained a preliminary conversion.

In a rather more sophisticated version—particularly after the past generation's experiences—essentially the same diagnosis and therapy continue to be propounded by liberals. They recognize that their rapid advance from the immigrant ranks has set the American Jews apart, as well as acculturated them. They did not spread evenly through Gentile society but concentrated in relatively advanced economic, social, and cultural levels of the structure; which, of course, aroused the hostility of the relatively deprived. As for those Gentiles who were found in the same social positions, they did not constitute a social milieu able to absorb Jews on neutral grounds. Religion or religious background continued to circumscribe their associations and a Jew, whatever his own preferences, was mainly thrown back on Jews. The key that unlocked other doors for Jews in secular America remained conversion.

But what did not work in the past may be working now, for the future. The particular spheres in which second, third, or later generations of American Jews have concentrated are also those to which current trends are bringing increasing proportions of Gentiles. Jews who followed the elite WASPs into the service trades, the professions, the suburbs, and the colleges—and who preceded them into the abstruse sciences and science-related industries—are now being followed there by other ethnic minorities, not to mention lower-class and rural WASPs. The attitudes of liberal tolerance which correlate with education and urban occupations and incomes are becoming increasingly significant in the weighted average of American opinion. The mass media, as well, have given wide currency to the metropolitan style, of which the Jewish liberal is an exemplary representative. The American Way, in short, is growing more and more Jewish.

What hopeful predictions could be made by projecting these undeniable trends is obvious. The conditions for destroying prejudice, according to the liberal analysis, are being gradually realized: education, urbanization, and incomes are rising, and relative deprivation declining, as Jewish-Gentile social and economic differentials are cut down. All this is happening, moreover, by an approach of the Gentiles to the Jewish norm, and not the reverse. This fact, which is often meaningfully pointed out, suggests to some Jewish liberals that a new milieu may be in the making that could absorb Jews without conversion. (They could also point to the sharply rising rate of Jewish-Gentile intermarriage, but it is more probable that this makes Jews Gentile than Gentiles Jewish.) A liberal American urbanized society, large enough and important enough to impose values on the consensus, may be developing which would be neutral to the Jewish-Christian conflict and immune to anti-Semitism. This is the utopia frequently hinted at but rarely proclaimed as an express goal or anticipation by today's Jewish liberals.

If few are inclined to make an ideology or express commitment out of this utopia, it is because neither self-hatred nor naïve optimism is feasible for the present generation of Jews. But this creates a situation of inner conflict. The wariness towards Gentiles and the defiant Jewish identity which are our weapons of last resort can be expected to appear in the last resort in the responses of contemporary Jewish liberals too; but in ordinary times such attitudes impose restraints which are constantly irksome to a liberal temper. The antithetical attitudes —that Gentiles may be trusted and that Jewish identity is unimportant—have a continuing appeal to liberals as personally liberating ideas.

The Jewish liberal is consequently predisposed to see evidence that anti-Semitism is sharply decreasing, that Gentile goodwill is reliable, and a solid Jewish-Gentile association on neutral grounds is increasingly possible. The gut may be perpetually alert for the alarm bell of genocidal peril, but the head is cocked for proof that the Jewish problem is becoming a negligible triviality and may safely be ignored.

One sociologist, Charles H. Stember, finds evidence of this kind in statistics on anti-Semitism compiled from public opinion surveys over the past forty years. The usual indices—fear of Jewish power, rejection of Jewish associates, strong (and negative) impressions of stereotyped Jewish traits—mounted sharply from the Thirties to the end of World War II. The debate over American involvement ranged Americans into sharply divided pro- and anti-Jewish groups, and reduced the moderate middle. Jews topped the lists of national menaces, being feared and hated more than the Japanese or Germans. But the war's end brought a precipitous and continuing decline in anti-Semitism —so measured, at least—which continued into the Sixties. (Negroes inherited the Jews' place as top American bogeyman after the war). Stember cautiously concludes that, if long continued—and particularly if considered in the light of the convergence of Gentiles on the Jewish urban, intellectual, and liberal way of life—this trend may portend the ultimate, real integration of American Jews.

Others are inclined to much greater caution. The same poll findings may be quite differently interpreted: they could well demonstrate that open, especially political anti-Semitism reminiscent of the Nazis was no longer respectable in America. People with anti-Jewish feelings no longer cared to express them in the kind of response currently associated with those who perpetrated the Holocaust and so recently threatened our own, as well as the world's peace. Other polls, directed for example to traditional religious rather than standard pre-War social, economic, and political stereotypes, showed a different picture. They highlighted, in particular, the regrouping of an apathetic middle that was not actively hostile to Jews but not opposed to anti-Semites either.

What has again challenged the liberal utopia was the recent, quite unexpected, recrudescence of the political anti-Semitic tradition among blacks, and some militant progressives of the New Left. There has been a rather desperate effort to deny the facts among liberals and in the Jewish establishment. Bitterly decrying the hysteria-mongers who play up reports of black anti-Semitism, they play them down in a panicky way themselves. They point to the low rates of anti-Semitic responses in opinion surveys among Negroes as compared with whites in the same social-economic categories. They note that Negroes fear relatively less Jewish political power (an index of genocide-prone attitudes?) and relatively more Jewish economic power; and that the latter hostility can be said to reflect direct contact with Jews, hence is not merely prejudice. But they ignore what is perhaps the most significant prognostic sign, from a liberal viewpoint, in this pattern: unlike whites, blacks show more hostility to Jews, rather than less, in the younger, better educated, more urbanized, and upwardly mobile group. The hostility in that group is more politically focused as well.

This aspect of the situation is, in fact, the most critical danger signal for a Jew in our time. The surface arguments among Jews about black anti-Semitism all skate on thin ice over a peril whose suppressed presence is tacitly understood by all. The unabashed anti-Jewish political attitudes taken by black militants have opened the door again for political anti-Semitism to gain an audience among people who consider themselves respectable.

BLACK AND WHITE ANTI-SEMITISM

The mere brute outcries of hate are less significant to the informed Jewish ear than more sophisticated slogans which pretend to be merely anti-Zionist, not anti-Semitic. No kind of anti-Semitism, from theological to political, disappeared after Hitler's defeat, but all—and particularly political anti-Semitism —found new code words for old hatreds in an attempt to remain respectable. The claim to be anti-Zionist, not anti-Semitic, was assiduously promoted by Arabs (and their barely tolerated Jewish coadjutors), while they did not cease at the same time to peddle the Protocols of the Elders of Zion and other hoary anti-Semitic libels. Nor did they dispense with the aid of sur-

131

viving veterans of the Nazi anti-Jewish apparatus who found service in Cairo in the same old cause. When the Russians (and Czechs, and Poles, and Communist East Germans) took up the gambit and embroidered it with their own slanders concerning the rootless cosmopolitan, Zionist-imperialist, Jewish world conspiracy, the code only grew more luxuriant and the associated league of Jew-haters more complexly opportunistic —but the anti-Semitic core remained.

None of these efforts succeeded in altering the major change in opinion that denied political anti-Semitism, however coded, respectability in the West. The recruitment of black militants to the "anti-Zionist" ranks threatened to do precisely that. As a material danger, black anti-Semitism may be relatively minor and it may also have relatively shallow roots in comparison with the Jew-hatred of the rest of the fraternity. But it threatens to accomplish—and not especially for itself, but quite as much, or more, for its allied political anti-Semites—what none of them could do alone: it immediately wins not only a hearing but a preliminary commitment to understand what was only yesterday a proscribed attitude, namely, raw, unlimited, political Jew hatred.

One may go still further. The anti-Semitism of black militants, and its reinforcement of Arab and Communist bloc anti-Semitism, has contributed to the rebirth of an openly self-hating Jewish liberal utopianism. In a neutral community of all who hate, each one his own establishment, some Jews now anticipate, as an automatic dividend, the resolution of their own identity problems.

This community of their dreams, too, has a peculiarly Jewish look: it is a community of dissent, not to say, of course, rebellion. For dissent, the Jew, alienated by birthright, is peculiarly qualified (as the black for rebellion), and any Gentile who joins assimilates to a progressive-Jewish mode. It is a resolution of the Jewish problem reached by a far different, an opposite route, from the hypothetical absorption of middle America into the metropolitan-suburban style of life; but it too is an authentic projection of the utopian Jewish liberal wish-dream.

*　　*　　*

As to these liberal utopias, it is fair to say that they are probably impossible in the ultimate sense, but have already altered the actual Jewish-Gentile relationship in a very marked manner. No true neutral community is likely to arise that can absorb the liberal Jew effectively while sparing him painful choices in regard to ethnic identity. But the cutting edge of ideological dissensus between Jew and Gentile has long been reduced to sponge by the growth of half-life, fringe communities of all sorts based on the confusion of identities. Not only liberal utopianism but intermarriage contributes to their rampant growth.

The theoretical requirements for a viable community in America that should effectively neutralize Jewish-Gentile differences include the following: 1) Neutrality towards Jewish-Gentile differences need not be its proclaimed principle, but must be clearly recognizable and fundamental. 2) The neutral community must be something as clearly defined as the West Indian mulatto, and not merely a pulpy membrane through which confused identities pass on their way to secure anchorage in the Jewish or Gentile communities. The question, in other words, cannot simply be avoided. 3) The neutral community must also be more than a fringe phenomenon. It must be recognized in the American consensus as permanent, not only distinct; and, to achieve this, it must be significantly large and possess a neutral subculture: a tradition, that is, which (by definition) passes down a chain of generations.

The two types of liberal utopia discussed earlier, which may be tagged for convenience the "establishment" and "alienated" varieties, propose implicitly to reach this goal by opposed routes. The first suggests that American Jews need merely hold still where they are and middle America will converge on their position. The problem not faced in this utopia is the ideological question: How, by simply standing still, will Jews achieve a clearly understood recognition that the liberal culture which urban America is to converge on is Jewish-Gentile-neutral and requires no betrayal of Jewish identity?

The "community" of the alienated is ideological enough, but shows little capacity to be more than a fringe phenomenon, and become permanent, not provisional, as a community. Jews are perhaps the only participants who now go into the alienated countercommunity with the idea of achieving their essential ethnic identity. To be for civil rights, the Third-World revolutionary conspiracy, and liberated sex, drugs, and foul speech is, they say, to be prophetically, primordially Jewish. But how long can this last? Can children be brought up in the "culture" of nihilism, to live by it as an institutionalized tradition? The notion is a logical contradiction in terms and psychologically self-defeating.

What complicates the issue today, though it mitigates the problem, is the unwillingness of contemporary American Jews to turn their backs on Jewish identity as readily as was done before Hitler, in France or Central Europe, for example. The issue of anti-Semitism remains a moral boobytrap barring all easy approaches to Jewish liberal utopias. Establishment liberals do not fully convince themselves with arguments that anti-Semitism is on the way out. Alienated liberals become unconvincingly shrill in arguing the distinctions which separate the coded Jew-hatred of the Third World from old-style anti-Semitism. The fear is barely suppressed in either case that utopia may involve one in a Jewish self-betrayal not tolerable to Jews today.

134

Anti-Semitism, which Jewish liberals not unreasonably see as the key index to questions of Jewish status, is a confused subject full of arbitrary definitions. The name itself is anachronistic for all but the racialist political movements, based on theories concerning the Semitic peril, which arose in the nineteenth century. But the underlying condition that warrants all the anguished attention given to the topic of anti-Semitism is far older and more pervasive. A variegated tradition of hating Jews exists that is specific, cumulative, and endemic, wherever Jews have lived in significant numbers: that is, in contemporary terms, among all Christian and Muslim peoples, and wherever Christianity and Islam have an important influence. This has repeatedly produced epidemic outbreaks, occurring in their most horrible form in the Hitler holocaust, the Genocide. This is what liberals seek to understand, as a single analytical process, in their diagnosis of anti-Semitism and in their therapeutic utopias.

The diagnosis is basically mistaken, and bears no true relation to the conditions that must be analyzed. If the utopias are so dubious, it is not simply because they counsel perfection, it is because they imagine ills which are not those we truly suffer.

*   *   *

Anti-Semitism, as Zionists used to say, may be a Gentile problem, but its causes are the Jews themselves. Jewish identity is tied to Jew-hatred in an indissoluble bond.

Hostility to the Jews is a necessary accompaniment of the tolerance extended to them as an ideological minority. They are tolerated, let us remember, because they cannot be submerged; not, at least, at a generally acceptable cost. The assertion of identity is ultimately a challenge to make martyrs of them; and, apart from the fact that the issues at stake have become totally confused in a liberal society which cannot see why anyone

135

should be martyred, the historical price of the "final solution" of the Jewish question was the totalitarian disruption and corruption of Gentile society. Reasonable Gentiles for past millennia did not need Hitler to instruct them that tolerance of the stiff-necked Jews was a law and order necessity.

As a defeated ideological group, Jews could be included in Gentile societies only by special measures of toleration; and in medieval Catholic countries, they were extended to them alone and to no others. Such an exceptional tolerated status is inevitably accompanied by a special irritable animosity. Not only were the Jewish privileges that were extended by central power resented by other subordinated groups and local authorities; those who gave the Jews an exceptional status necessarily adopted a wary, suspicious attitude in the very act of granting it. Jews protected by law were also restricted by law or customs in a way calculated to protect Gentiles against the ideological contagion implied in their very existence. Tolerance towards the Jews necessarily had as its reverse side a hostility and suspicion, present from the beginning and accumulating over centuries and across continents in a tough, enduring, complex, variable, and highly flexible tradition.

It is pure folly to imagine that this can be dissolved while Jewish identity remains. But it is equally misguided to construe a straight line of development from anti-Semitism to genocide or from tolerance to integration of the Jews. The tendency to make this assumption has led, especially since Hitler, to a neurotic, if not paranoid, attitude to Jewish questions—which, of course, require higher than ordinary tension even for normal adjustment. The kind of tempered hostility in Gentiles which Jews must live with and recognize as natural, if they are to remain Jews, arouses a paranoid frenzy in some, who discern portents of a new Hitler, and sets off a neurotic repression of consciousness in others, who refuse to see any anti-Semitism that does not bear definite genocidal implications.

In fact, however, throughout history attitudes of hostility to the Jews never formed a single continuum up to and including the motives that prompt genocide. Nor did tolerant attitudes favorable to the Jews constitute a continuous set up to and including those necessary for "integration"—whatever that fuzzy word really means.

A clean gap separates Jew-hatred from genocide, and another separates toleration from integration; and, in each case, a specific set of circumstances, not simply the normal strain of Jewish-Gentile relations, is needed to explain the leap across the chasm. Tolerance together with anti-Semitism constitute a single ambivalent attitude indissolubly connected with the historic Jewish situation. As opposite poles of the same syndrome, they stand of course in inverse proportion to each other, so that anti-Semitism increases as tolerance declines and vice versa; but we are dealing with new phenomena, not to be understood in the same terms, when the sphere of ambivalence is exceeded and either hostility or acceptance is no longer limited by its opposite. Genocide destroys and true integration could only abolish the historic Jewish identity.

Anti-Semitism is thus perennial, so long as there are Diaspora Jews, as is tolerance. This applies to pre-Christian, Christian, and post-Christian times, and of course to all countries with a Muslim tradition. The theologico-ideological clash gives clear meaning to the Jewish identity among believers, but it also defines the basic condition of the no-longer-believing Jews, while in many cases confusing their identity. This situation is universal for the entire extension and duration of the Diaspora.

There are also special expressions of anti-Semitism, related particularly to the significance of the Jewish question in national or ethnic histories. France (except Alsace) and England were virtually without Jews from the high Middle Ages to early modern times, and both American and American Jewish history are entirely modern. Hence, when Sephardic Jews began to

137

settle in those countries there was no more than a generalized anti-Semitic tradition of prejudice against them. In Central and Eastern Europe, on the other hand, Jew-hatred was nourished by continuous contact with Jews degraded by law and tainted by the illegitimacy of their tolerated presence and activities in the eyes of the mass of Gentiles. In France and Germany, but not in England or America, the emancipation of Jews became a cardinal symbolic issue in the left and right partisan division of national politics and cultural history. What form anti-Semitism took and, in particular, how it was politically used in each of these situations varied widely.

It was a common feature, in any case, that the emancipation of Jews could not have the same effect as the emancipation of Christian minorities in a Christian country. America, to take ourselves as an example, developed its way of life on secular principles, like other Christian countries, in terms of a national language, literature, life style, and political tradition and history; but in its basic ethical and, so to speak, metaphysical commitment it remains Christian, if not Protestant. Catholics may contest the last specification, because they, too, are Christian. Jews dare not; and they prefer not, because to do so would only land them in a more specifically defined Christian and less nearly secular society. They have, in other words, the choice between a situation in which anti-Semitism is more fully covered by tolerance and one where tolerance is more explicitly limited by anti-Semitism; but not the utopian option of a society totally neutral to Jewish-Christian (ultimately, ideological) differences.

Another widespread feature of the Jewish situation is the availability of anti-Semitism—including the readily mobilizable and easily expansible anti-Semitic network, as well as its multifarious tradition—as a flexible instrument of widely different political purposes. In mid-nineteenth-century France, the left made use of anti-Semitic prejudice no less freely than the right; and when, after a considerable period of silence, the Marxists finally decided to condemn anti-Semitism, "the socialism of fools," it was only because they feared it was seducing the workers out of their own ranks. Some rightist demagogues, notably Hitler, were lunatic fringe anti-Semites themselves, while shrewdly manipulating traditional Jew-hatreds for political advantage. Others, however—Vienna's Lueger and von Schoenerer, Berlin's Stoecker, and Detroit's Father Coughlin—were notably cool and rational in their use of this weapon, stepping up the pitch of their agitation in response to its demonstrated effectiveness.

Black anti-Semitism, especially in the form of black nationalist militancy, conforms to the last pattern. It is quite correct when Jewish liberals defensively argue that the primary Negro hatred is hostility to whitey, and that anti-Semitism is a facet of this greater hatred. When blacks make Jesus a Negro it is intended primarily to deny that he is white, rather than to deny he is Jewish, as in the Nazi neo-Christianity of the Aryan Jesus. One of the forms of antiwhite, anti-Christian black militancy is precisely certain Black Jewish sectarianism.

But anti-Semitism gives Negro militants a specific advantage: it is one way of joining the big battalions, a source of strength and numbers. The advantage is not only material, though the funds, contacts, and other tactical and strategic supports black nationalism may gain by espousing anti-Zionist anti-Semitism are not insignificant. The advantage is psychological as well. It ranges from the simple satisfaction of being in the majority Christian religious culture to the more heady exhilaration of joining the Third World as it rises in its numberless hordes to swamp the iniquities of the Judeo-Christian world-history and world-empire.

Whether it appears as a rational calculation or a compensating emotion, political anti-Semitism presents a difficult and urgent problem of judgment to Jews. Particularly when it takes the current coded form of anti-Zionism, it may represent no more

139

than the rational political exploitation of a convenient weapon. The objects of its use, by non-Arabs especially, may not even be primarily to extract advantages from Jews. Soviet anti-Zionism, while venomous enough in its anti-Semitic animus, has in mind the United States, Europe, Africa, and Asia as much or more than the Jewish problem in Russia or in Israel. Negro anti-Zionism certainly has other fish to fry than the problem of Israel's fortifications on the Suez Canal; and in the Third World united front, where black nationalists bring their anti-Zionism as a cheap free-will offering, they make quite sure to demand full, preliminary acceptance of their own demands and direct interests—not from Israel or the Zionists, but from anti-Zionist, New Left Jews.

To the extent that anti-Zionism uses anti-Semitism as a matter of expediency, rationality might suggest treating the issue in terms of the end, not the means. The Jewish movement most inclined to do this is the Zionist movement. In its classic period, under Theodor Herzl, political Zionist leadership sometimes proposed to deal with outright, undisguised political anti-Semites in precisely this way.

Zionism is based on rejecting the Diaspora Jewish situation radically, and refusing to respect the limits of the tolerance-anti-Semitism syndrome. It proposed to transcend the Exile neither in the direction of integrating nor obliterating the Jews, thus abolishing the misfortune of their distinct identity, but by liberating them in their homeland to realize their own destiny. But such a solution, they supposed, might well be negotiated with anti-Semites, who also wished a conclusive solution of the Jewish problem; at least, with those of them who were coolly and rationally anti-Semitic, as some of Herzl's Viennese contemporaries were.

But even on cold, rational grounds anti-Semites may well conclude that it is easier to obliterate the Jews than to release and liberate them in order to get rid of them. In any case, anti-Semitism as a tactical method, as a weapon, no matter how coldly and rationally used, is essentially a mania. Whoever makes use of it lets loose a fury that knows no limit, that can truly expend itself only in genocide and not in any more limited way.

Within the ambivalent syndrome of Gentile attitudes that permit or sustain Diaspora life Jews can, and must, put up with anti-Semitism. It is normal in Exile and must be normally faced: that is, ignored or disdained or opposed or strenuously resisted as the occasion requires. Political anti-Semitism in all its forms, and however coded, raises possibilities transcending tolerance. Its most natural conclusion is genocide, and the forces it conjures with are genocidal in nature.

There can only be one adequate Jewish response: immediate, unequivocal resistance. Whatever Herzl may have thought, Eastern European Zionists, the authentic fathers of the movement, knew this thoroughly and implicitly from the first pogroms that gave Zionism birth. They knew then what the Holocaust has taught us all: resistance is the ethically essential, the only adequate as well as the only possible, response to the genocide implicit in political anti-Semitism in any form.

141

VI.   The Ethnic Revolt

As dissent is the implicit threat inherent in the very existence of the Jewish minority, so disobedience is the danger always feared in the black minority, even when Negroes are most passive. Both perils to the majority have now become actualities to be faced; and the share of the classic minorities in them, while far from being exclusive or, perhaps even predominant, is nonetheless impressive.

That disobedience should be associated with Negroes is easy enough to understand. They are a social minority whose essential relation to the whole society is one of oppressive institutional subordination. Their objective condition invites revolt.

One might add that they were originally an agrarian labor class and were concentrated in the culture area of the Southern United States. On both counts their propensity to violence could be assumed with good reason to be great. The impulsive brutality of rural areas does not enjoy the same careful reporting and accounting that produces our urban crime statistics, but the atrocities committed there are familiar both in literature and history. The Old South, so tellingly exposed for us by W. J. Cash, is a major source of the culture of violence which, a young black leader recently noted, is as American as apple pie. Thus the majority culture, as well as the pressure of their own oppression, implanted a high potential for violence among Negroes in America.

The fruit of such a soil and nurture did not fall ripe from the branch in the South, for continual repression is a well-tried method to tame the resentment that oppression breeds; and no

142

scruples were strong enough in the South, itself resentful of Northern self-righteousness, to inhibit the requisite harshness. The fruit of violence rotted on the tree and dropped seeds of bitterness inherited by succeeding generations. When the two World Wars brought large waves of Negro migrants to Northern and Western cities, the indiscipline combined with the brutality of the slums gave violence opportunity and occasion for the explosions we then witnessed.

The city slum, or the "ghetto," as it is now called, adds its own virulent ingredients to the countermorality of ethnic violence. What Oscar Lewis calls the "culture of poverty" is strongly in evidence, most notably in its pathologies, in the contemporary ghettos. The sway of crime, backed by political and police corruption, and the grip of vice on a population sick with self-hatred and ridden with those maladies bred in broken homes by deposed or abdicated father-figures: such conditions, common to all immigrant slums, attacked a people in the black ghetto whose resistance was already undermined by their earlier background.

One of the elements strongly evident in the thinking of some contemporary intellectuals, going beyond their ethical appreciation of active resistance to oppression, is the attraction plain violence has for them. The conventional morality of civil obedience and civic cooperation, resting as all civilized behavior does on the repression of unruly impulses, has always produced a countermorality in the young and untamed and among the poor, who pay for but rarely enjoy the civilities that uphold society. There are times, and ours is clearly one of them, when civilization is bought at such a price that sensitive men— especially, overcultivated men—reject it as unreasonable and intolerable. They then discover the ethics, and also the charm, of the people's spontaneous rages and furies, and they applaud bloody violence as a necessary temper tantrum, therapeutic for the repressed; or, in the more desperate cases, they throw themselves into the revolutionary orgy as a personal release and liberation. Under these circumstances what exists in every disrupted, disorganized, disoriented slum or *demimonde* as a "culture of poverty" is elevated into a new philosophy of revolution, and those who would otherwise be simple hoodlums are transformed into leaders of national revolutionary causes.

These remarks, I hasten to stress, are not entirely ironic. Certainly a Jew, whose people's long history of passive resistance never rested on illusions about the absolute ethical value of meekness and weakness, must appreciate the ethical imperative of resistance to evil, of active self-defense; for it was one of the special torments of our Exile that the ethic of active resistance was so rarely possible for us, because so generally it would have been suicidal. Resistance came to mean for us who lived during the Holocaust the last refuge of our humanity. It signified the final assertion of freedom, the freedom to die by our own choice, when faced with certain death. If we hope to build a future that post-Holocaust Jews can tolerate, it will be by guarding the freedom to resist when life and what makes life worth living, and not only a more honorable death, may be won thereby.

The ethnic revolt of the Jews, which took place in Eastern Europe, where Jewish masses were an oppressed social as well as ideological minority, an impoverished underclass or interclass as well as an alien religion, produced its own appreciation and attraction towards tough, violent, or simply underworld figures in the community. Not only Zionism but the whole activist mood of Eastern European Jews arose from a powerful revulsion against the pious, patient endurance of Jews in Exile awaiting Redemption. "Freedom now!" was their cry too, and their heroes were no longer martyrs, but rebels and revolutionaries. The noble figure of young Gershuni, the Social Revolutionary terrorist leader, of the Zionist avengers Dashefsky and

Schwartzbard, were paralleled in literature by Zalman Schneour's and Isaac Babel's enthusiasm for earthy, simple, violent, and criminal Jews, who neither knew nor cared for the ancient tradition of penitential suffering, but returned a blow for each blow.

There was, no doubt, a certain innocence about the early enthusiasm for violence of some Jewish revolutionaries and nationalists. The terrorist proclivities of young Jews, whether as amateur in the craft as many young Zionists or as professional as some young Social Revolutionaries, were far more effective in building morale and myth than for immediate tactical ends. Only in the final clash with the British before the creation of Israel can the claim be made (though on highly disputable grounds) that terrorism was an historically effective Jewish political weapon. The major significance of direct, retaliatory action here too remained its psychological function: it was a release for intolerable emotional pressures that were felt by all Jews during the years of horror; and sympathy for the terrorists extended well beyond the wide circles of their committed supporters. But this was no longer innocence. The violence of Jewish activists during and after the Second World War was not capricious, but expressed a grim and deeply personal necessity. And whatever one may say of their strategy, Jewish activists and terrorists certainly developed a high proficiency in the tactical use of violence.

Violence is not merely a pathological outlet for individual frustrations, hostilities, and aggressions in any society. Violence is normally institutionalized in the limited force of authority under the law and the customary excesses of authority figures under cover of law; in the more or less covert pressures that accompany collective bargaining on the side of industry and labor alike; and in the countermoral rule of the peasant mafias, slum gangs, and rackets that regulate major parts of the infrastructure of our real world. All this takes place in a world in normal balance. Even the violence of international warfare is conceivably part of such a balance.

Violence is also widely understood to be a necessary element in producing fundamental social changes. While Marx himself is fairly uninformative on this point, Marxist theory since the master has had as its main preoccupation and casuistical problem the endless debate over correct and incorrect applications of force in the social revolution. Violence, in this context, becomes not only an ethic or a therapy but a pragmatic political technique.

* * *

The secret of "scientific" revolutionary violence is the combination of a mass base with a dynamic idea. Whether or not such a combination is successfully achieved depends on the relations of intellectuals to the particular mass bases upon which, in their local environment, the revolution must stand. In some respects both Jews and Negroes are similarly handicapped in the relations of their intellectuals to the mass, but it is apparent that the Negro situation is more conducive to an ethnic combination for revolutionary violence than is the Jewish situation. This is true even when one makes the proper comparison—not between American Jews and Negroes, but between blacks in America and Jews in Eastern Europe.

There is a tendency in any minority for the ambitious to try to solve their status problems by assimilation, by identifying with the majority. Jews and Negroes, like all other minorities, suffer defections because of this, particularly marked among the upper middle class and intellectuals. But Jews and Negroes are also outstanding among that group of American minorities whose assimilation is restricted within fairly rigid limits. Neither

146

the Jewish nor the Negro problem in America seems likely to be solved by full absorption; and, in addition, when blacks or Jews seek to solve their individual problems in this way, they fail, unless by passing or conversion, to achieve a full resolution. They succeed, however, in confusing their own sense of identity and threatening that of the ethnic community.

Full absorption, then, is denied even to those who defect from their ethnic identification, if they do not pass or convert. This is true for both Jews and Negroes; but there is a large and important margin of difference in the degree of partial absorption available to Jews and blacks. Jews, not only in America but in densely settled, ethnically aware Eastern Europe, could gain far greater acceptance and live a more nearly adequate life as marginal types than is available to the black American intellectual or bourgeois even today. For blacks, only in the Caribbean or Latin America—or perhaps, by expatriation, France—is there an equal chance for the same kind of partial absorption.

One consequence of the availability of a partial kind of integration was that Jewish intellectuals who turned revolutionary were likely to direct their energies outside the narrow ethnic fold and identify with the local Gentile mass base. One might go further. There is a distinct tendency for Jews to be prominently represented among those revolutionary thinkers whose attachment to *any* local mass base is highly tenuous. Marx, Trotsky, Rosa Luxemburg are all theorists on a high plane of abstract excellence; and their detachment from the basically ethnic realities of their revolutionary moment in history, most obvious in the old master himself, is no less evident if one compares Luxemburg to Lenin or Trotsky to Stalin. If there were Jews, however, who developed tactical skills and the necessary sense of concrete realities, they frequently applied their eminent talents in some non-Jewish ethnic field. Ferdinand Lassalle, whose youthful Jewish ardor was chilled by the

147

submissive response of the community to the 1840 Damascus ritual murder libels, became the grandfather of German Social Democracy.

The outlet of general revolutionary activism is, in principle, available to the rebellious American black, too, but it is far less likely to be used. He finds his base for action, together with a new, secure sense of identity, in the revolutionary potential of the black ghetto mass.

There are also similarities and significant differences in the propensities of the Jewish and Negro masses towards revolutionary activism. It should be noted that, apart from a few merchant colonies of Sephardic Jews, the European Jewries and overseas immigrant communities, mainly recruited from Eastern Europe, presented social problems after their emancipation not unlike those of the emancipated blacks. They came into modern industrial civilizations from the outside and at the bottom. Liberals who favored their cause did so in the face of grave, general doubts, which they partly shared, about the Jews' capacity to become men of humane culture, economically productive, socially compatible with Gentiles, or even loyal fellow citizens. Where not discriminated against on these nominal grounds, as in Western Europe and America, they were oppressed politically and economically, as in Eastern and Southern Europe, on the grounds of being a dangerous alien element. Most Jews came into their new civil rights as a poverty-stricken, unskilled, uprooted, and ill-treated *Lumpenproletariat*. The present-day black ghetto, in these respects, bears a close resemblance to the Jewish (and other ethnics') immigrant ghetto of the late nineteenth and early twentieth century.

But there is also a clearly marked difference. Whatever the causes, it is a striking fact that once emancipated, Jews with remarkable speed made all those transformations needed for successful functioning in modern industrial civilization. In their cultural and economic achievements, their political identification, indeed, in every way but the final social integration required for full absorption, Jews outdid the fondest hopes of their liberal friends. This was true of Alsatian Jewish peddlers in France, and also of the Ashkenazi Jewish mass in Central Europe, from Germany and Austria to Poland and Hungary, to the extent that they were emancipated. It was notably true of Eastern European overseas migrants who in the United States achieved a greater rise in the usual categories of social and cultural advancement—that is to say, of adaptation—than any other ethnic element of the contemporaneous New Immigration and, for that matter, than other ethnics with the advantage of a generation or two of Americanization behind them.

The effect of emancipation in a modern industrial environment was practically to cancel out the Jewish masses as a base for revolutionary activity. There was a major attempt (by the Bund) to organize Jews ethnically for the revolution during the early industrialization of Eastern Europe, but its success was limited to the period *before* Jews were emancipated. The 1917 revolution that finally emancipated the Jews also crushed the autonomous Jewish labor movement. A far more consistent and enduring ethnic-revolutionary synthesis was carried out by the labor Zionists, but they operated neither under conditions of emancipation nor of an advanced industrial society. They liberated the Jewish nation by emigrating to the backward agrarian wasteland of Palestine. The only Jewish labor movement to work under the postulated conditions were the Jewish trade unions and radical parties in America and a few other Western countries.

Their commitment to revolutionary ideologies was as ardent as any, but by the second generation successful adaptation of the immigrant Jewries had cancelled any ethnic revolutionary potential. Radical leanings were still relatively strong among Jews, but many were no longer workers. They could provide sympathizers and intellectual leaders but not a mass base for a

149

revolutionary movement. Those who remained workers had gained security with the increase of skill, including an outstanding skill in trade union organization. Whatever violence was left in them was part of their adaptation to the normal balance of an open or semi-open society.

The contrast with the Negro situation is plainly evident. The Negro migration to the industrial cities, long after their emancipation, is now two generations old, but is still in flow. What the final accounting will show remains to be seen; and we may well be in for some surprises, particularly in regard to individual achievements of the highest quality. But it is certainly clear that the adjustment of emancipated Negroes to their movement into modern industrial civilization has encountered serious difficulties which are at the heart of today's critical Negro problem.

The contrast with the Jewish situation is one of which black militants are acutely aware. One of the frequent themes of their argument is the need to build on what they assume to have been a major Jewish advantage: the powerful clannishness, the self-esteem, and the active, organized mutual aid and commitment to ethnic interests attributed to the Jewish community. These, they contend, underlie the morale which, among other benefits, has enabled the Jews to achieve their outstanding adaptation to the challenge of America.

The lagging adaptation of Negroes to industrial society has, on the other hand, left them eminently available as a mass base for revolutionaries, given a suitable method to activate them. The revolutionary potential of the Negro mass was first tapped not before their emancipation (as with Eastern European Jews) but long after, with their introduction into a modern industrial environment. Their ethnic interests are today accepted not only by their own intellectuals but by whites in the revolutionary movement. Their radical potential exists almost solely on the base of the American local situation; and whatever small

150

movement back-to-Africa existed was poles removed from the radical commitment that played such a significant role in Zionism. Finally, there seems very little chance that, in the near future, the economic and social problems of the Negro mass will be resolved by individual adaptation, either to middle class status or to the security of organized labor.

RADICALISM AND ETHNIC INTERESTS

The conquest of the proletarian radical movement by Marxism meant, in principle, that the way was blocked for any fair approach to ethnic interests by social revolutionaries. The only nation the Marxist vision recognized was the proletariat itself, as the forerunner of a new international mankind. In his analysis of current political issues, Marx favored or disqualified peoples according to their likely contributions to the proletarian revolution. Generally he approved of advanced industrial nations like Germany (with reservations) and disapproved of agrarian nations like Russia (hence the support for Polish nationalist revolutionaries); and he generally approved of big nations with large territories and major economic resources and disapproved of small peoples, let alone landless, dispersed minorities.

In spite of these prejudices inherent in Marxist "scientific socialism," not to speak of Marx's own bias, subsequent major developments in Marxist doctrine were often produced when revolutionary situations made it necessary to recognize specific ethnic interests and situations hard to reconcile with the system. The roster of Communist saints counts, after Marx-Engels, the original pair, Lenin-Stalin-Mao-Ho- and possibly, some day, Tito, Castro-Guevara, and Nasser-Sabri: all men who introduced new theses into the party canon particularly suited to their own local condition.

Jewish radicalism, stemming from Eastern Europe, also ad-

151

justed Marxist orthodoxy to its own needs, or drew on non-Marxist social revolutionary ideology. Even the Bund, whose ethnic commitment was most inhibited, began with the contention that separate ethnic organization alone could or should give Jews their fair share in the benefits of the revolution. They crystallized their final stand in the principle of "personal (exterritorial) autonomism," claiming for all Jews in a socialist Russia rights and facilities to maintain their ethnic culture in their national tongue, Yiddish.

But the Bund ignored the main theoretical problem which the specific condition of the Jews presented to any Marxist. The Jews were not proletarians exploited by an advanced industrial system. They were mainly middlemen, the *petite bourgeoisie* of a backward agrarian system; or, if they were workers, they were craftsmen or sweated labor in small, precapitalist, or retarded capitalist, workshops and home industries.

Those who squarely faced this problem were the socialist and radical Zionists, a small group with innumerable ideological variants. Some at first held that political activism in the Diaspora was neither possible nor desirable for Jews. Others, somewhat later, agreed that the revolutionary struggle in the Diaspora was not relevant to basic Jewish needs, but they held it to be essential both for self-defense against anti-Semitic reactionaries and as a point of honor. Still others for a while believed that in order to accomplish the planned mass migration and territorial concentration needed to build a Jewish state, the essential prerequisite was to attain by political activism full rights and a reconstructed solid social organization and economic position in the Diaspora. All were agreed on one point: that the Jewish problem would truly be solved only when an independent Jewish labor society was established in Zion. All, too, addressed themselves to the immediate problem which the Jewish situation presented to radicals and socialists: how to reconstruct the abnormal economic situation of the Jews.

This was a twofold task, with immediate and ultimate objectives, carried out in the Diaspora and in Zion by the same essentially constructive methods. It aimed to abolish the degradation and poverty of the Eastern European Jewish masses by cooperative organization and vocational retraining and by planned emigration and resettlement in Zion. The settlement in Zion would from its inception be based on mutualism and ethnic and international brotherhood and would build up organically a just and classless, prophetic society; or, in a Marxist variant, it would produce a true proletariat, in the wake of the capitalist development and industrialization of Palestine, which would permit Jews for the first time to participate normally in the class struggle and social revolution. What, in either case, typified the ethnic quality of Zionist radicalism was the importance assigned to social and economic constructive processes, to vocational retraining, planned migration and resettlement, to investment and to social organization, at the expense of the usual overwhelming commitment to the immediate political goals of radical militancy.

The constructivism characteristic of labor Zionists was generally shared by Jewish radicals active among the Eastern European mass in the late nineteenth and early twentieth century. In America it produced innovations in trade union practice, most fully developed in the needle trades, and in Palestine the inventive social and economic institutions of the Histadrut network by which the whole structure of Israel is decisively shaped. In America this enabled trade unions to help significantly in the individual Jews' adjustment to an advanced industrial society. In Israel it built major sections of the groundwork and structure of the whole society in a strongly mutualistic spirit.

*　　*　　*

When the situation of blacks in American cities occasioned revolt and gave black radicals their opportunity, they too had to improvise positions adapted to ethnic needs. Historical coincidence led them to adopt many tactical expedients and, above all, catchphrases and ideas rooted in recent Jewish, particularly Eastern European, experience. But the objective nature of their situation demanded and led to a far different basic approach.

The more truly a Jewish radicalism responded to the ethnic situation, the more fully it detached itself from the whole society and sought a autonomous solution for Jewish problems. Jews sought freedom and social justice by emigration and resettlement in an independent ethnic society in Zion. For American Negroes nothing is more natural than to seek a solution of their problem where they live, and moreover to present the programs obviously demanded by their own ethnic situation as a proposal for radical change in the values of the whole society.

It is obvious, not only to blacks, that if there were no racism, there would be no oppression of Negroes; and, some say, no "Negroes" at all, as the category is a mere myth of white racists. The simple solution of the Negro problem is, accordingly, that whites should stop being racists. The proposal for a radical change in white values flows directly from the basic ethos which whites share with blacks.

For this reason, the first real Negro revolt was not the violent episode of Nat Turner; nor the militancy of Marcus Delany or Monroe Trotter or W. E. B. Du Bois, which expended itself in debate; nor even the mass adventure of Garveyism, which barely related itself at all to white America. Martin Luther King produced the first effective national activist movement among Negroes. His method was the use of passive resistance —not as a way of life and survival, as among Jews in Exile or enslaved blacks, but as a Gandhian technique of mass political action.

This was a revolt whose ideology invoked and tactics relied upon the values of the very Christian civilization against which it rebelled. The program of action was to compel by law and

154

moral pressure what the white world ought to grant freely under the principles of justice and charity it professed to live by. The full measure of King's demand—integration into white society—involved not only the white conscience, which might be compelled, but the gift of love, which can only be free. It was King's and Gandhi's insight that love, too, has something in it that seeks to be compelled, and a common faith, or even a common humanity, is a fitting reason to compel it. (But it is a different matter when, in the name of a common humanity, one insists not merely on tolerance but on love wholly renouncing hatred so that a *religious cleavage* may be bridged. When Jews demand theological reforms of Christians, or Negro athletes boycott a Mormon football team in protest against religious doctrines, it seems more like belligerency than militancy.)

One cannot deny that King's campaigns and other pressures of the same sort have achieved great advances. The belief that integration must be enforced so that brotherhood may be learned, rather than the reverse, has not only gained widespread acceptance but—in spite of setbacks and backlash—has had appreciable success when applied. The direct attack on public opinion, in campaigns to assert the Negro presence and project black dignity through every channel of communication, has been extraordinarily effective. We can already register a change in stereotyped attitudes to Negroes no less remarkable (and perhaps no less superficial) than the American popularity of the notion of "our Judeo-Christian civilization."

But what would be achieved practically if this program were completely successful, and white Americans accepted blacks without reservation as together and equal? What it might mean would be opening up to Negroes the same opportunities for partial absorption that are available to the Jewish intellectuals and upper middle class. In effect, one may say, this has been virtually accomplished. But what has not begun to be accomplished and what does not seem likely to be achieved by this approach is successful individual adjustment to modern industrial society like that which raised the mass of Jews from the slums to the relative security or moderate affluence of their present position.

Few suggestions are so infuriating to black leaders as the proposal that they should lift themselves by their bootstraps as it is assumed other minorities, and notably the Jews, have done. They angrily and scornfully point out the glaring differences between the two cases. The Negro masses are the product of four hundred years of slavery and oppression; robbed of culture, emasculated by oppression, their pride and solidarity broken. These conditions deprived them of vital advantages which, in their view, Jews began with: literacy, ambition, the habit of mobility, a fund of skills and capital, and a strong communal organization traditionally prepared to employ these resources in aid of the Jews. But the conclusion they then draw is that the black revolution must provide Negroes with the Jews' initial advantages: not only education, but ethnic pride and a powerful ethnic organization. They state similar conditions, moreover (in a manner reminiscent of the reparations claim made good against Germany by the Jews), as a direct political demand on the white community, which must provide special educational facilities and large, freely disposable capital funds to the blacks in compensation for centuries of captivity and exploitation under slavery and peonage. But given these prerequisites, it is sometimes tacitly assumed, the mass of Negroes individually would climb the ladder to well-being as Jews did.

*   *   *

The question whether the conditions underlying Jewish economic adjustment are correctly understood in this description deserves to be considered directly. The Jewish community is neither as well-organized nor as efficient as the argument assumes. Only a minor fraction of the Eastern European immigrants to America before 1920 owed anything to communal assistance; their major institutional supports were a tight family solidarity and the neighborly aid of earlier immigrants who came from the same part of the Old Country. But what is of more interest is the role of the individual Jew's ethnic self-image in his effective adaptation to modern society.

Leaving aside Sombartian or Weberian speculations about the effect of the "Jewish spirit" or "economic ethic," it is clear that those qualities and capacities essential for the survival of a tolerated ideological minority under any other conditions are equally, if not more, suited for adaptation to advanced industrial civilization. A tolerated group of dissenters, however noncombative (that is, East Asians in Africa or Chinese in Malaysia as well as militant Puritans in seventeenth-century London or Amsterdam), does well to keep its assets in readily convertible and transportable form, as it may have to pull up stakes and find a new refuge at any moment. Such groups have good cause not simply to be merchants, craftsman, or service professionals of a kind readily employable anywhere, but also literate, self-reliant—and driven—men. Having no place in society such as is institutionally allocated to those who share in a consensus of belief, they must find their own place within the tolerated area of their freedom. They accordingly have, in general, a strong "need-achievement"—a will to succeed.

It is hard to imagine anything black nationalists could do to reproduce this background. Even if it were possible, they would hardly wish to share the long experience of alienhood and restrictive toleration that made Jews so adaptable to commerce, services, and the professions.

There is also a clear morale-building element in the mere ideological distinction that constitutes such a minority as the Jews. In their case, the religious doctrine of chosenness and the grand mythos of Exile and Redemption explicitly indoctrinated attitudes of special obligation which were reinforced in the minutely detailed commandments of the tradition. Even without such discipline any ideological commitment that sets one apart in principled dissent implants a sense of excellence and a need to excel. The constant awareness that one is tolerated rather than accepted, that one is watched, that one must prove oneself, produces in the conscious dissenter an alert and wary concentration, a high-strung compulsiveness. It calls for strength—weakness under this strain becomes neurotic—and if strength is there, it leads to a maximum accomplishment.

Black militancy is converting at least part of the American Negro community—or the whole community partially—into something approaching an ideological minority (just as the growing identity confusion of American Jews is moving them to the position of a social minority with no more than a mythic subculture). One conscious aim of the black revolutionaries is precisely to indoctrinate pride, ethnic self-respect, and personal morale into the Negro *Lumpenproletariat*. That this *is* the effect of a black nationalist program on many of its members is proven by a wide range of cases, from the Garveyite and Father Divine days to the Black Muslims and, now, perhaps, the Black Panthers. The reformation of pimps and pushers and the growth of manly self-reliance are common incidents in the history of the effect each of these had upon its members.

How far can this therapy go? Can it, for example, bring about such a wide-ranging regeneration of the apathetic, hopeless, and disoriented mass of "ghetto" blacks that they will be motivated, as Jews were, to meet the challenges of an urban, industrial society successfully? If one were to believe this possible, one would have to imagine a black nationalist culture as broadly shared and profoundly experienced as Jewish culture once was among the Jews. The great hold of the nationalist mood upon American Negroes today reflects the fact that they are in a quasirevolution; and collective uprisings always create broad, powerful currents of collective solidarity. What they do not immediately create, except for the cadres of the completely committed activists, are profoundly regenerating values which decisively form identities. Only the long persistence of institutions born in the revolution does this.

The ordinary American Negro could be personally motivated to achieve as the ordinary Jew was only if his whole people, and not an activist minority, became permanently, and not for an interval of crisis, cast in the mold of an ideological minority. The ethnic awareness of the moment does not in itself satisfy the conditions necessary to produce such motivation.

Other important conditions of the Jewish adaptation are also unavailable to American Negroes today. I have referred to the family ties and neighborly mutual aid societies that were primary supports for the green immigrant. Their adjustment to America was also greatly eased by the fact that a number of industries, of subsidiary importance to the growth of the industrial cities, were Jewish specialties, built on the investments and management of older Jewish settlers, and employing skills especially developed among the Jewish immigrants. Jewish employers, in other words, not the undifferentiated American economy, gave Jewish immigrants their first foothold in the New World. The case of Israel illustrates the point even more clearly. An organized effort of Zionist radicals created whole classes and economic sectors, a Jewish agricultural economy and a Jewish rural and urban working class, which did not previously exist in Palestine, and were hardly characteristic of the Diaspora Jews who came.

Neither in America nor in Palestine did the adjustment of Jewish immigrants conform to the pattern of the first employment of many of them. But the later pattern, too, was in both cases the product of Jewish initiative, not of simple absorption into an existing, general economy. Sons of Jewish industrial laborers in America moved into commerce and service trades and, by preference, into self-employment, opening up in many cases fields relatively untouched by the established economy. The Jewish immigrants in Palestine moved out of the labor settlements and other Zionist-sponsored sectors of the new Jewish society but built unplanned extensions of what remained a separate Jewish economy quite loosely attached to the old Palestine that preceded them.

The current black nationalist movement in many respects adopts or seeks to apply similar methods, but their circumstances severely limit the extent of possible success. The black community, having been a fixed part of the established economy for so long, has no tradition of self-sufficiency in the ordinary, housekeeping details of their own local economy. Relatively few of them make a living by the common expedient of serving the others, while a comparable group, the Puerto Rican immigrants, have not only their own barbers and numbers runners but a whole range of local services, from grocers to doctors and lawyers, of their own. The black nationalist campaign for greater economic autarky in the ghetto is a natural response to this situation. Nor is this economic nationalism limited to the ghettos. There have been equally reasonable efforts to build up more self-sufficient black towns, ranches, and villages in rural sections.

How effective can such a program be? The difficulties that face such a constructive radical nationalism are appalling. Anyone who has visited black areas recently evacuated by white merchants must be dismayed by the rows of boarded-up, unused storefronts. The Goldbergs are out but the brothers have not stepped in to perform the functions they served. Nothing like this is conceivable in a Puerto Rican quarter, not to say a Chinatown, with a population long identified and internally integrated by its own, fully elaborated ethnic culture.

The huge morale lift of ideological nationalism may rehabilitate wasted lives. It may even, as Father Divine did, build up in its own ranks the elements of greater economic autarky. But to apply in this way the methods which produced such spectacular results among Jews in Israel, or Jews in America, will not solve the desperately pressing problems of the mass of big-city Negroes today. The whole general economy, and not the separate economic constructions and strategies of the minority, must be looked to for solutions on this scale.

*　　*　　*

The general economy, in fact, was the agency by which all newcomers were expected to be absorbed and were indeed absorbed into the advanced industrial society of America. The standard pattern of economic succession, assumed generally by American historians, describes the native WASP stock as a body of restless pioneers who opened up frontiers and then left them for development and consolidation by more stable types, like German or Scandinavian farmers. When industrialization gained speed, their native-born population moved upward on the social ladder, leaving room on the lower rungs for immigrant Irishmen, Italians, Hungarians, and Slavs. The expansion of the general economy generated a need for large labor forces. Their number and character were regulated, under pressure of the established trade unions and WASP nativists, so that the organized, secure laborers would not be undercut and the Old American style of life would not be threatened.

A superficial examination of this pattern makes it obvious that it cannot meet the needs of Negroes today. However similar their problems, Negroes newly arriving in American cities are not foreign immigrants. Their numbers are not controllable according to the needs of the established economy, as the rate of foreign immigration could be. They are Americans, and their movement within the country does not come under any Immigration Act. What draws them to the cities are not only jobs

161

left unfilled by other Americans, as with immigrants. They also seek other opportunities—better schools or welfare grants, for example—open to them more generously in one part of the country than another.

The fit between demand for labor at the bottom and the supply of foreign immigrants may have been imperfect but was fairly close at all times. Immigration rose and fell with employment. For the Negroes this equation simply fails to account for major elements in their movement to the industrial cities. The result is unemployment, underemployment, and the massing in ghettos of large, floating, disoriented, and embittered Americans.

They are also politically armed and activated Americans. Like many immigrants they are driven to move by oppression at home, but they come in a totally different spirit from the foreigners. Immigrants looked to American freedom with hope and fear, prepared from the outset to conform to unknown demands of the land of opportunity. Migrant blacks come to industrial cities from the rural South with clear conceptions of their rights as Americans, bitterly determined to wrest them, if necessary, from a reluctant North.

ETHNIC REVOLUTIONARIES

Neither of the two classic minorities, Jews and Negroes, falls well into the standard pattern of social and economic succession by which newcomers are expected to be absorbed into the real America. There is evidently a close relationship between the reasons why they are not fully assimilable and the reasons why they do not flow smoothly into the upended bottom of the American economic barrel.

The Jewish adjustment to this problem, successful as it has been for individuals, was achieved fundamentally by a method of separation and avoidance, reformulating in subtle, attenuated

162

forms their universal position in Gentile society. They did not truly enter into the established social and economic structure, becoming integrated in their assigned positions within it; they rather negotiated the structure like an obstacle course, circumventing its restrictions and avoiding its fixed channels, to find a place for themselves in its zones of expansion and free growth. A similar method, which in America was of course highly apolitical, achieved for Jewish emigrants to Palestine the political triumph of a national home, an independent Jewish state.

However attractive this approach may be to black nationalists, and however useful its results in certain important respects when they apply it, it is basically unrelated to the primary needs of the black community and to the main direction of their authentic impulse. The movement natural to American Negroes, who are fundamentally a product of American history, is towards greater integration; and even many of their separationist demands, like black studies departments in white universities or black community control in school districts within a white municipal or state administration, are integrationist in method and often dialectically integrationist in goal. Their fight within the system to be freed from it always requires taking the whole system with them to their destination. Even their separatist violence knots them in a closer clinch with the opponent. Their methods, therefore, must necessarily be both political and revolutionary.

The adjustment of Negro migrants to the industrial cities quite plainly requires methods directly at odds with the American liberalistic tradition. This goal will not be achieved by *laissez-faire* procedures. No well-tried methods guaranteed to succeed are known for such a task, but even to undertake it implies a diametrically opposed approach. Preferential quotas in employment; preschool reading-readiness training, Upward Bound programs, and open enrollment at universities for Third World minorities; integration through enforced racial balance

163

by busing children, together with segregation by black community control in school districts or on college campuses: all such proposals imply accepting, together with the goal of equality for Negroes and other certified disadvantaged groups, methods to achieve it which may deny equal opportunity, advancement by merit, and the free choice of their associations to others, and which may also be logically inconsistent among themselves.

We have seen all of these demands not only advocated but in some cases won. While it is far from certain that a real revolution is under way, let alone that it will fundamentally alter all our institutions and the values underlying them, radical changes directly at variance with our old values have been institutionalized in parts of our social structure.

Many changes are such that the direct appeal to common Christian and American values of a Martin Luther King could not have brought them about. His brand of nonviolent militancy, his appeal to conscience, to the Bible and the Constitution, could logically lead whites, abandoning racism, to renounce explicit discrimination and racial segregation. Such demands were consistent with a purist adherence to the very values white America professed. But a demand for separatist autonomy, for a segregationist black nationalism, and for preferential status for blacks in educational and employment opportunities was not consistent with such values; it required their abandonment and the institution of new forms of nationally pluralistic, neosocialist equity. King's school of thought could not consistently have formulated nor were his methods likely to have attained these objectives. They require an ideology prepared to lay down and a tactical doctrine prepared to impose demands flatly at variance with the common white-black Christian American values.

Revolutionary demands and methods entail the activation of mass impulses not just of masses. Peaceful moral demonstrations, expressing the faith of a leader like King, might wring reluctant concessions out of guilt-ridden whites, but only such

164

concessions as lifted a deep-rooted sense of specific guilt. He could force them not to be racists and stop offending their own conscience by discriminating against God's children, their fellow Americans. When demands of another kind were made, openly rejecting the liberalistic tradition of the American consensus, guilt helped soften the will of white America but only alarm at clear and present dangers bent it to the point of yielding. Bombing, burning, and rioting brought about the degree of submission to separatist, black nationalist programs of special preference that we have seen (together, of course, with the equally significant degree of white backlash).

Any revolution that activates masses necessarily unleashes the ungoverned impulses and suppressed desires of the people themselves, not those prescribed in the ideological manuals of the leaders. The leadership cadre of a revolution counts on exploiting the force of mass impulse at the revolutionary moment, and then cutting it off when it has done its work. But the black revolutionaries are far from being a leadership cadre of intellectual ideologists. They themselves embody the mass impulse, giving it a highly eclectic, loosely fitting ideological cover for the confusion of authentic intellectuals. Every revolutionary tactic since Lenin has made concessions to the special needs of a particular people, and many revolutionary leaders were, like Stalin, Khrushchev, Mao, or Nasser, earthy men, men of the masses. In few cases, however, has what claims to be a revolution sprung as directly from the mythic springs of an oppressed people's resentment and been as little restrained by ideological strategies as the current black militancy.

*　　*　　*

The special doctrinal innovation of the black revolutionaries is their reliance on the *Lumpenproletariat*—to put it plainly, on politicized street gangs and rehabilitated criminals—as the

165

chosen instrument of the revolution. They pick up in this respect a tradition of the Black Muslims and of Malcolm X; but they cover it with the psychiatric neo-Marxism of Frantz Fanon. Through him they understand the gang violence and mob action which is part of their culture of poverty to be not only a therapeutic catharsis but a necessary stage in the political dialectic of their revolution. (A recent Black Panther "constitutional convention" also approved of "drug culture" as a temporary aid to revolutionary consciousness.)

The gangs, transmuted into ideologists, have accomplished a major social transformation of the Negro community in making their bold bid for leadership. They have forced the Negro intellectual and middle class into greater conformity with the values of the ghetto mass. By taking the initiative for communal causes, and converting gang warfare and mob actions into political tactics, they have compelled the established leaders to defend them, and even to accept certain of their objectives, if not their methods. There has been a rehabilitation not only of street fighters through the conversion of a countermoral culture of poverty into a revolutionary ideology. If the ghetto activist has gained a new ethnic identity, so too has the detached black upper class. They are now black far less because white society offers them no adequate channels for absorption, and far more because the ghetto demands from them a serious commitment and offers a significant identity.

The point at which activists from the *Lumpenproletariat* and militant black intellectuals meet is a New Left type of black revolutionary ideology. Both in its Old Left Marxist background and in its immediate New Left milieu, this brings Negroes into a particularly pointed love-hate relationship with Jews. It is the point of infection out of which arises the current intoxication of black anti-Semitism.

Anti-Semitism among Negroes is rooted in the universal position of Jews as dissidents in a Christian (or Muslim) world;

166

but like all other kinds of anti-Semitism it is also colored and focused by the special experiences of Negroes with Jews. As in so many other of their relationships, Jews often live at the point of immediate contact between black and white communities. Just as they ran the estates and dealt with the Ukrainian serfs of the Polish *szlachta,* so Jews ran general stores or peddled in Negro areas in the South and remain to trade in Harlem and other ghettos once inhabited by Jews when Negroes have taken them over.

Zones of contact between groups in conflict are also zones of friction. The anti-Semitic stereotypes of Negroes faithfully reflect the particular frictions of their direct contacts with Jews. The images of the avaricious and deceitful and dangerously powerful Jew are the same as those of other Gentiles, but the special Negro experience determines which of them are most salient and gives them a new format. Negroes, in general, are much less likely than American whites to fear Jewish power in politics, and more likely to stress instead Jewish economic power. The age-old Shylock image becomes, in Negro city folklore, Goldberg, the slumlord, the extortionist storekeeper, and his wife, who hires the *shvartze* cleaning woman off the street or at the employment exchange.

This is anti-Semitism at its chronic, normal level. Not only is it without the tripwires and complicated international connections of political anti-Semitism, but it sometimes approaches the down-to-earth quality of ordinary ethnic prejudice. Negroes, who until they became militant did not readily voice any of their antipathies, even today show a consistently lower average response than white Americans to the usual survey indicators of anti-Semitism. For the silent majority of Negroes there are other enemies much more salient and significant than Jews. Moreover, the awareness that Jews are hate-objects of their own antagonists is widespread and still emphatic in the Negro mind.

The black ideological militant is quite another matter. That hostility to Jews becomes more intense and politically focused among younger, better educated Negroes is surprising only as a sociological observation; historically considered, it can be readily understood. It expresses the specific experience of militant Negro intellectuals and ideologically involved black militants with the Jews in their own zone of direct contacts.

The Jew these black activists meet in a personal encounter is not Goldberg in the ghetto, but the Jewish leftist or liberal in the Communist party, the civil rights movement, or the New Left. For James Baldwin it is Norman Mailer, for Harold Cruse it is Herbert Aptheker; Stokely Carmichael, Eldridge Cleaver and many, many others all had their Jewish friends and comrades who were devoted sometimes to the point of ultimate sacrifice—but who also never hesitated to point out to blacks just what it was that blacks had to do.

This is a common Jewish role in many modern revolutions, and it has a very common outcome. Stalin had his Trotsky and his Kamenevs, Zinovievs, and Radeks, and Khrushchev often complained in various formulations of too many Abramovitches. In the very beginning of Russian Marxism, the Russian Social Democratic Party was, in large part, the creation of the Bund, founded shortly before. Both the Bund and the Jewish Bolsheviks, who were at first highly prized leaders of socialism, were ultimately erased with a decisiveness that owed something to the resentment of Jewish domination, and was not simply the penalty of false doctrines. Stalin's Judeophobic "doctors' plot" and the campaign against "rootless cosmopolitans" in the Soviet Union and the satellite countries, continuing in various forms to the present day, revealed openly the anti-Semitic quality of the pervasive, indigenous anti-Jewish hostility of Eastern Europe. That it tied in, from the 1950's, with a growing Soviet antagonism to Israel and reliance on Arab nationalism made the old-style "Protocols of Zion" stereotypes of an international Jewish conspiracy even easier and more convenient to adopt.

One of the first effective political organizations available to American Negro intellectuals was the Communist Party. It gave them what had been a vaguely felt but painful lack until then: connection with a mass movement—indeed, one global in its scope—and with a dynamic plan of action. Without this connection, effective action had been monopolized by the Booker T. Washingtons and the Negro ward-heelers, who worked within the severely limited tolerance of the white political establishment, both North and South. Marcus Garvey organized an autonomous Negro mass movement by opening up to blacks large vistas of imaginary ethnic action which united them with the countless millions of their African brethren; but he neither faced the realities of a white world in serious confrontation nor provided any political strategy that an intellectual could accept. He was, indeed, outspokenly anti-intellectual. W. E. B. Du Bois, the antagonist of both Washington and Garvey, long sought to attach himself to the Pan-African antiimperialist cause—that is, to a global-scale mass movement—but only when he became a Communist was he able to join an apparatus that could be taken seriously as an effective political force.

Negro separatism in America became one of the progressive nationalist ideas that the Moscow hierarchy decided to look on with favor; and the American Communist Party took it up as a promising point of entry to a potentially revolutionary mass. A number of Jewish Communist scholars and ideologists became leading advocates of this idea; they developed a considerable expertise, and virtually converted the field of American Negro Marxist history and the Communist activation of the black masses into a personal specialty. At least, this was the way things seemed to such a young black Communist intellectual as Harold Cruse. He sensed that the Jewish Communist

169

hierarchs were stifling the spontaneous nationalist impulses of black comrades by their ostensible, purely tactical, support of the cause; and in this he was unquestionably correct, for the Jewish Negro experts were orthodox Communists, who supported nationalist ideas for their immediate revolutionary effect and in the expectation of wiping nationalist deviations out in the era of the new Soviet man that was to follow. But Cruse also suspected them of something more. In his eyes they were Jewish nationalists, favoring a Jewish autonomy in the Party they would not concede to Negroes.

In Cruse, who is a paradigm for numerous successors among the current cadre of black militants, what developed was an acute, very pointed Judeophobia, a strongly hostile ambivalence towards Jews, especially Jewish radicals, who demanded his respect and threatened his pre-eminence in the very areas that meant most for his own identity. Fanon has said that the authentic, minimum revolutionary demand of the wretched of the earth is quite simply "that the last shall be first." This, quite simply, is what the intellectual revolution Cruse projects is all about. Not Jewish nationalists, posing as Communists, but Negro revolutionary nationalists are to determine the goals and methods of the revolution; and methods and goals are to be derived from the specific situation and spontaneous impulses of the black masses in America, both in the immediate phase and ultimate resolution of the historical dialectic. The analysis and direction of the whole process belongs legitimately to the black intellectual.

Not all black activist leaders who today take a similar position are intellectuals, but quite uniformly they share the same psychological situation vis-a-vis their Jewish radical comrades. The liberation of black militancy by the black power insurgents was signalized by expelling whites from the civil rights movement; and "whites" in many minds meant "Jews." The reconciliation of black militants with white radicals took place in

170

1967 in a highly significant and interesting manner. First a conference of blacks adopted a thirteen-point program of revolutionary nationalist demands; then a black caucus, comprising about ten percent of the Chicago New Politics Conference, demanded, and obtained, acceptance of their program and effective control by themselves of the whole Conference as the condition of their participation. The last had become first, with *éclat*.

But an equally significant feature of the reconciliation was that the "first," too, had been demonstratively made last. One of the features of the black thirteen-point program was its anti-Zionist plank. This was not only an inheritance of the black power contingent from Malcolm X; it gave them, as it gave him, the material support and the sense of global relevancy which an attachment to an international political alliance could provide. It tied them to Third World and Afro-Asian blocs and opened up options of several Communist alignments, with advantages of prestige and substance. Now, in the *rapprochement* with the American New Left, the anti-Zionist plank of the black program had a latent function, as the sociologists say: its objective effect was to force on the significant Jewish element at Chicago in 1967 a formal act of implicit submission. New Left Jews who bowed to the black nationalists' demands had to seal their surrender by spitting in the face of Jewish nationalism. Nothing could make clearer the reversal of imputed roles or more directly compensate black leaders for the humiliation of their sense of Jewish dominance in the civil rights movement.

The demand to be self-proclaimed anti-Zionists was one for which American Jewish radicals were not yet prepared. The unanimity of American Jews in support of Israel had its roots in a common traumatic revulsion against Jewish defenselessness, such as had seared the minds of all who had witnessed the Holocaust. This experience brought together in consensus many

171

who had accepted no clear commitment to the ideology underlying a Jewish state, or who were even, in principle, opposed.
For many of the latter the passage of years and the successful
establishment of Israel made it possible to relegate the whole
issue of Israel and of Jewish survival to the level of a minor
concern, if a problem at all. Others, born after Hitler, did not
experience the Holocaust era as a personal trauma, but as one
of the hang-ups of the parental establishment. Even they, however, preferred to overlook the whole matter of Israel, rather
than take an ideological stand on it.

The New Politics Conference took place in the midst of a
revived awareness of Jewish exposure to genocide and a re-
newed Jewish pride aroused by the Six Day War, its prelim-
inaries and aftermath. The brusque demand to take a formal
anti-Zionist position was for Jewish radicals a true crux, a test
of allegiances central to identity. Those who then said Yea
committed themselves implicitly to a postliberal utopia: the
revolution was affirmed as a collective and personal identity
by the obscure and devious expedient of endorsing black
nationalist anti-Semitism. Others, who said Nay, now faced the
need to make their reasserted Jewish identity something significant enough to justify the courage of their own break.

VII. The Emancipated and the Liberated

IT is natural to discuss American Jews and American Negroes, as I have done, in terms of comparisons and contrasts. So much about their position and problems is alike, that what is unlike is all the more striking. To produce aphorisms and paradoxes on this topic is easy; but one should not therefore assume that the parallels and oppositions intuitively grasped are too obvious to be significant.

Looking back at what has been said, the temptation to dismiss it as superficial is great because the rhetorical structure is so pat. Jews and Negroes may be the last major unassimilable groups. But while very few Negroes can pass no matter how much they may want to, any Jew who wants to, in principle, can. Jews and Negroes are classic types of the oppressed minority, and in America they have a common interest in civil rights and brotherhood. But the oppression of the Negro for the meaningless fact of his color is unsanctioned by "normative" American culture—to borrow a phrase from the Jewish theologians. His appeal to be accepted, even to be loved, is solidly founded on the Christian civilization he shares with white Americans. Jews' oppression and separation constitute a mutual relation, rooted in a religious opposition, centuries old, that radically divides Jews from the Gentile world. No matter how the rivalry is muted and transformed, it raises an invisible barrier that keeps them out because they themselves would not pass it. The Jews, and not only the Christian world, have invested their differences with high value.

These paradoxes and antitheses are old, and the passage of

173

time does not make them sound more profound, only staler. Yet the situation they describe has not radically changed, in spite of some stray contrary indications; and while the phrases become more commonplace with time, they have not become the less true.

Another parallel is the relation of emancipated American Jews and Negroes to Israel or to Africa, where the liberated brethren of each minority exercise sovereignty in their several nation states. One of the cardinal features of both the Jewish and Negro situation after emancipation in America is their problematic and confused identity image. The new relation to liberated Israeli Jews or black Africans highlights this problem for each emancipated community—and, some may hope, could contribute significantly to its definition and possible resolution.

Here again we are confronted with a pat and paradoxical comparison. It was always considered a remarkable fact about Jews that their ethnic aspirations were centered for thousands of years on a land they no longer possessed. If the creation of Israel represents the national liberation of the Jewish people (which only the blindest partisan will deny), then the people liberated continues in its overwhelming majority to live in the Diaspora. How to reconcile the needs and experience of emancipation in the long-established Diaspora with the needs and experience of liberation in the newly created Homeland is one of the fundamental Jewish difficulties of the present time.

What was considered a unique experience of the contemporary Jew has now happened also to the contemporary Negro. After a century of the history of the emancipated, or quasi-emancipated, Negro in America, we now see the rise of numerous liberated black nations in ancestral Africa. How this presents identity problems, as well as a focus for identification, has been shown by Harold Isaacs, especially for Negroes returning to Africa, in a close parallel, as he has also noted, to a similar problem of some American Jews returning to Israel. The differences between the two cases, however, are even more striking.

Israel was created by a Jewish nationalist movement which originated in the Diaspora, was conceived as a solution for the Diaspora Jewish problem, and had much of its history, culminating in the foundation of the state, in the Diaspora. Israel exists because emancipated Jews in Western countries and, more importantly, not-yet or no-longer emancipated Jews in Eastern and Central Europe believed they needed it for their national freedom or, in the extremity, for their survival, for their lives and safety. In the long, complex struggle and the final convulsions of resistance and warfare that produced Israel, the Jewish settlers in Zion at all times depended on crucial support from the Diaspora, and particularly on the active help of emancipated Jewries.

Liberated Africa has no such relation to the American Negro. The liberation of African nations south of the Sahara in no way depended on the episodic history of Negro nationalism in America. Neither in fact nor in conception does it solve the ethnic or personal problem of black Americans. Accordingly, the significance of liberated Africa for American Negroes and their predominant response to it is sharply different from the significance of Israel for American Jews and their predominant response to it.

There are, of course, complex and subtle variations of the American Jewish response to the rise of Israel. Yet one may venture the rough generalization that the dominant tone in the reactions of Diaspora Jewry, especially in America, was one of a great release.

Arthur Koestler, as previously noted, put the point with a biting sharpness. For him, the rise of Israel cancelled his obligation to be Jewish. Until Jews were liberated as a people in Israel, he argued, Diaspora Jewry was an embattled army, un-

175

justly beset by foes, and only a renegade or a coward could desert the ranks. Honor required loyalty even if one had little or no belief in the national cause and battle slogans. (In other words, the Jewish people was arbitrarily oppressed as an ideological minority and, when threatened with extinction, was entitled to the solidarity of those Jews who no longer accepted or understood its ideology.) But Israel has arisen and the national existence is now secure in its hands—or, at least, Israel now bears the responsibility for Jewish survival. To continue to be a Jew in the Diaspora under these circumstances requires personal belief in the cause and slogans; and anyone who lacks this has been released from duty and may honorably depart.

This is, of course, an exceptional view. Most Jews in the Diaspora still feel unable and also unwilling to decamp. But for them, too, the creation of Israel has meant a significant release; not always, however, a pleasant one. Many, sharing Koestler's outlook without his frank decisiveness, accept their Jewishness as an existential fact, but an empty and, since Israel's rise, an unimportant one. At least, that is their attitude until something like the Six Day War revives the dormant Jewish reflexes of solidarity and self-defense implanted by the Hitler experience. On the other side, those Diaspora Jews who had most clearly identified with the role of political combatants for the Jewish people, the Zionists, also experienced a sudden release. All at once, and totally unprepared, they were relieved of the responsibility of creating the Jewish commonwealth. Together with it they lost the sense that, in the absence of a sovereign Jewish polity, they, the Zionists, represented the general will and self-determination of the Jewish people: in what they did, or failed to do, the Jewish people was tried and judged by history. The release from this testing duty was also a severe shock to their sense of identity.

The American Negro generally felt no personal responsibility for the survival of his community as an ethnic entity. Not even black nationalists, of whom until recently there were relatively few, would necessarily entertain such an attitude. To the extent that American Negroes were an ethnic block, it was clear to everyone that this condition was imposed on them by white oppression. The ethnicity of African blacks certainly did not depend on American Negroes. Marcus Garvey and W. E. B. Du Bois, to be sure, had some influence on such a leader as Nkrumah, and each in his own way looked to a future in which Western blacks would inspire and lead Pan-African nationalism. But these were individual, if not eccentric, wish-dreams, neither widely shared nor effective.

Hence the liberation of black African nations in no way released American Negroes from earlier duties of conscience. It was, if anything, a challenge to take on new obligations, to demonstrate a new ethnic commitment. The explosive upsurge of American Negro militancy, even though it sprang directly and authentically from immediate American conditions, has an unmistakable connection with the challenging example of the liberated African nations. Its effect extended to those Negro leaders who were staunchly committed to integration as well as to black separatists. The new sense of ethnic identity which buoys up a community-wide solidarity clearly owes something to the inspiriting experience of black liberation in Africa.

The challenge of liberated Africa was thus also a unifying force in the emancipated slave community of American Negroes. Among postemancipated American Jews, a general commitment to the building of the Jewish national home had been shared by consensus ever since the times became critical in the Thirties. The unity on this point continued after the Jewish state was founded, though the intensity of commitment fell and rose with the ebb and flow of threats to Israel's survival.

But just as Zionism had raised divisive issues involving Jews' definition of their identities, so liberated Israel implied such problems, in a way inconceivable in the relations between

177

the liberated and the emancipated blacks. Some of the implied problems were easily soluble in a purely formal way. Thus, not only the fringe-group anti-Zionists of the American Council for Judaism but the American Jewish Committee, operating within the consensus, openly raised the question how American Jews were to be spared any imputations of "dual loyalty" arising from their sympathies and attachment to Israel. The problem was readily solved. Israel gladly issued the formal (and quite gratuitous) statement the Committee desired, that the Jewish state represented and spoke for its own citizens alone and not the world-wide Jewish people; for Prime Minister Ben-Gurion had reason to stress the converse proposition: that only citizens of Israel, and not Jews abroad, however legitimately concerned with Israel's policies as well as its welfare, were entitled to share in the exercise of Israeli sovereignty.

The Jewish and Negro situations are not only analogous and strikingly contrasted. They are also continually coupled. Both the liberated Jews and the liberated Negroes, on the one hand, and emancipated Jews and emancipated, or quasiemancipated, Negroes, on the other hand, are involved with one another in a fateful and sometimes disturbed relationship. One can say with some confidence that the liberated Jews and the liberated Negroes can succeed in defining their relationship in a reasonable and mutually helpful way. It is harder to say this of the Jewish and Negro communities in America.

The Israelis have always been acutely aware of the extraordinary, indeed uniquely exceptional, character of their restoration. A landless people might, in theory, be entitled to reclaim its land, especially if they found that they could no longer survive as a people in any other way. But in practice such a theory would probably not be recognized by another people in long possession of the land, and would have to be established by every available means of conviction. From the beginning Zionists hoped to reach their goal by peaceful penetration; for their whole traditional

178

Jewish behavior pattern, the moral quality of their claim, and the tactical imperatives of an essentially weak initial position demanded such an approach.

The final stages of the Zionist triumph had ultimately to be won by force, by desperate self-defense in the face of intransigent Arab hostility; and the state had to be defended once and again in nearly continuous warfare. Even Israel's peaceful relations with neighboring neutral states demanded constant care and protection in the face of the Arabs' continued denial of Israel's legitimacy and the political and economic campaigns to undermine it.

Israel's relations with African states are invested with distinct echoes of this moral and political situation. The old Zionist feeling that the moral integrity of their movement would be demonstrated in the social and economic benefits accruing to its neighbors reasserted itself in relation to African and other states, with whom Israel had no political quarrel. The special pride of a national liberation movement whose utopian socialism had proven itself in constructive achievement made Israelis feel it to be their mission to help other newly liberated nations, by precept and example, to make a go of freedom. Such a humane extension of their nationalist ardor in its natural arena, the Middle East, was to have sealed their acceptance by the Arabs. With this possibility closed to them by a rigid barrier of hate, they sent missions of technical assistance to Asian and African and, recently, Latin American countries. Not only did these lands represent a substitute outlet for their ardor to teach, but they offered Israel its best chance to break the circle of hostility the Arabs sought to close around it.

Among the countries where Israel figures as a technical mentor and aide, new African nations are foremost. The specific advantages for them in getting such guidance and help from Israel rather than larger, more powerful countries are obvious and have been many times noted. But one should not overlook

179

how easy it would have been for the African nations to fall in completely with the facile stereotype of Israel as a neocolonialist stooge of imperialism, a bridgehead of white aggression, to be classed with Portugal or Belgium, if not with the Union of South Africa. Margaret Mead, at an early stage, also speculated that Israeli economic initiative in Africa would touch off one of the most deep-rooted and universal anti-Semitic stereotypes, the Shylock image.

What prevented such developments, or held them in check, even though they surely lay along the path of least resistance, was the sober and reasonable spirit in which Africans and Israelis alike managed their relationship, as between sovereign peoples. In technical assistance planning they have worked out a remarkable symbiosis, one of close cooperation carefully avoiding meddlesome interference. Israel's economic assistance is initially offered or requested with clearly understood procedures, safeguarding African sovereignty and stipulating the method of Israel's ultimate withdrawal from part ownership or control.

The same well-regulated friendliness governs Israeli-African understanding in touchy areas of general politics. Each side knows clearly in advance the special political interests and circumstances which the other cannot afford to ignore. African states expect and receive, as a matter on which conscience rather than interest determines policy, Israeli support on anticolonialist measures—for example, vis-à-vis South Africa—but accept the limits which Israel's vital interests impose on some of its votes. Israel, on the other hand, lives with the hard necessity of seeing African nations—particularly those deeply involved in Pan-African politics and dependent on Egyptian-Algerian support—vote resolutions in support of Arab stands that verbally threaten her vital security, and then explain privately that such public postures need not disturb their friendly working relationship with Israel on development projects.

Such an Israeli attitude, and the limitations and difficulties to which it is subject, reflect the new position of a sovereign Jewish community in relation to the universal menace of anti-Semitism. In spite of the Zionist theory that anti-Semitism would expire with the end of Jewish homelessness, everyone can now see that it has survived and, indeed, that political anti-Semites make the Jewish national home their prime contemporary target. Israel is in the same position and under the same moral pressures as Jews everywhere in the face of this menace. It can oppose no less than immediate and absolute resistance to the genocidal threat, whether resistance means defending its own vital interests or endangering them for the sake of Jews imperiled elsewhere.

But Zionism, and certainly its fulfillment in Israeli sovereignty, redeems Jews from the thrall of anti-Semitism at least in one important respect. The uniformly passive resistance of the Exile was a specific acceptance of anti-Semitism as the ruling circumstance of Jewish life. Traditional beliefs relieved Jews of the need to adjust themselves in continual defensive actions against anti-Semitic dangers; anti-Semitism was a constant, not a variable, and, above all, it was an instrument of Divine policy. Zionism allowed Jews both to defend themselves actively against variable anti-Semitic aggressions and, like the traditionalists, to ignore it as fundamentally not their own but (in this case) the Gentiles' constant problem. Nevertheless, living as they did as a minority among Gentiles, anti-Semitism was a pervasive fact, and likely to be involved in any conflict that required Jews to act. Only in the state of sovereignty, in Israel, are Jews able effectively to distinguish between threats requiring action within normal limits, like those involved in any ethnic clash, and the threat of genocidal anti-Semitism requiring the specific, absolute style of action which is its only appropriate response.

*   *   *

Until recent years everyone assumed *a priori* that Jews and Negroes in America ought to have not merely a reasonable, friendly relationship, like the liberated Israelis and Africans, but something more. At present this is hardly the case. Not even a reasonable, friendly relationship exists, let alone a bond of brotherhood and alliance, except for select groups of Jews and Negroes. The foundation upon which rests the notable achievement of Israeli-African symbiosis is the fact that both parties involved operate from the base of sovereignty. Each has a highly developed regard for his own independence—not just his freedom, or civil rights and liberties, but his dominion, his control of and responsibility for his own actions. Just this is lacking in the case of Jews and Negroes in America; and lacking mainly because of the inherent difference between liberation and emancipation.

There was a time when ethnic self-interest, clearly shared, gave the Negro and the Jewish minority a basis for rational cooperation in common demands upon America. The breakthrough to nondiscriminatory policies in employment, the universities, and public accommodations appeared at a time of national emergency and a pressing need for all manpower resources and skills in World War II. Taking advantage of this need and of a wartime mood of national brotherhood, Jewish and Negro organizations, and notably the NAACP and the American Jewish Congress, jointly fought through a series of antidiscrimination and civil rights measures.

But then the paths diverged and underlying oppositions came to the surface. The Jews had suddenly achieved the goals of their own interest and reached a high level of adjustment on the liberalistic basis of merit. The Negroes still were at the first stage of the needed adjustment and it was already apparent that liberalistic principles would not be enough. Their new demands were such as to threaten the fairly achieved position of others by changing the rules of the game.

182

In the face of the opposition that had emerged, Jews were no longer able to respond by consensus and in the rational light of self-interest. Their communal organizations, built to fight discrimination and aid immigrants, were increasingly nonfunctional for a native-born community of men who had economically and socially arrived. Jews themselves were increasingly confused as to the nature and grounds and the interests of their own identity. Above all, they were severely inhibited from any effective action as a community acting either out of broad statesmanship or rational self-interest, for to act as a single community seemed to many Jews to place barriers in the way of their integration in American society.

In the event, they responded to Negro demands not as a consolidated community but each segment after its own Jewish identification and self-image, refracted in a dozen different ways by the prism of their several adjustments to the real America, the WASP majority. The result was almost always a distortion. The synagogues, Jewish welfare agencies, and national civic organizations showed strong schizoid traits. Some, reflecting their authentic traditional function as service organizations of a tight ethnic group, could find no role for themselves in struggles that did not advance, or even counteracted, clear Jewish interests. Others pursued their old liberal principles, but on the basis of new assumptions. They took their adjustment so seriously that they imagined that they could behave towards Negroes like majority Americans—that is, white Christians if not like WASPs —not like a Jewish minority. They then demonstrated the falsity of their premise by their failures.

Not Jewish values but Christian values underpin a consensus that could, theoretically at least, fully absorb American Negroes. Nor can Jewish welfare agencies or synagogues act effectively like Christian missions. Philanthropic altruism is never a truly useful social attitude when fundamental problems are at stake, but Christians, at least, can carry it out consistently. In principle they hold out to those whom they uplift the promise and right of full brotherhood. Jews altruistically involved with other minorities cannot offer them the full acceptance of ethnic absorption into the synagogue, unless they on their part accept conversion. The case is more likely to be reversed: the price of such altruistic brotherhood for Jews is often the surrender, if not defamation, of their own identity.

This, the most pernicious consequence, is not uncommon among far-out post-Jewish militants committed to Third World causes. Some civil rights activists specifically interpret this commitment as the whole of their *Jewish* identity, which would otherwise be totally empty and meaningless. But this circumstance, which defines their personal plight, does not make them more acceptable or their role less obnoxious to the oppressed minority they commit themselves to. Philanthropic altruism is always resented by its beneficiaries as patronizing. Combined with the usurpation of militant leadership, such altruistic dedication to other peoples' causes (common among romantic Englishmen as well as marginal Jews) seems like the denial of autonomy, pride, manhood, and freedom to the intended beneficiaries. The consequent resentment leads to the most pointed, personally grounded, and politically oriented anti-Semitism to be found among American Negroes today.

It need hardly be added that the disorganized Jewish community cannot deal rationally with anti-Semitism, including in particular Negro anti-Semitism. The most thoroughly confused, who have sunk their whole identity in the commitment to black-led revolution, accept the consequence of self-hatred. Others, at the opposite end of the spectrum, see anti-Semitism where there is none and react to all anti-Semitic manifestations as if they carried the genocidal menace of political anti-Semitism. Defense against anti-Semitism has long been institutionalized as the special function of professionals and organizations;

and their different approaches to the problem, reflecting varying kinds and degrees of adjustment to majority America, are not oriented to ethnic self-interest as defined by an active consensus. Only a critical emergency brings that consensus into effective operation.

The most common approach to Negroes in the liberal Jewish establishment still remains the assumption that, as brother minorities and not merely fellow-Americans, Jews and Negroes have a common cause. In spite of the obvious oppositions that now exist, the Jewish community still feels called upon, and *is* often called upon by Negroes, to make a special contribution: not just the contribution demanded of all whites, and certainly not the contribution Christians must make, but the special contribution Jews, with their special historical memories and present problems, ought to make.

The demand assumes that American Jews are something themselves, as a collectivity, integral and self-determined. If they were, they would be capable of dealing rationally with the patent oppositions between Jews and Negroes, in a spirit of enlightened self-interest, and not in the unwanted and self-defeating role of altruistic meddlers. But is the Jewish community indeed capable of doing what is asked? Just this is today in question, owing to the advance of Jewish integration.

The point is quite simple and quite concrete. Jewish organizations cannot, for example, take a principled stand on civil rights and social welfare issues as a single community unless they are a single community. For many purposes, however, they are not a single community; and this is so precisely because of their unwillingness to place barriers in the way of their integration with American society.

Nevertheless, if Jews are to give the justly expected, specific Jewish response to Negro demands, they must clearly and cleanly assert in this matter a single collective Jewish identity.

185

This, too, is a demand justly made of any emancipated group which is precluded by considerations of honor and conscience, and not by insuperable barriers, from complete assimilation.

* * *

Only liberated peoples, who do not want to integrate but only to coexist in equality, can achieve a reasonable, mutually agreeable, contractual relationship of symbiosis with others, including after a due interval their former rulers. People who are only emancipated cannot expect this and, when all the consequences are clear, they may not want it. For a rational integration cannot stop halfway; only by submerging an emancipated group, only by enforcing their total submission, can any society fully integrate them. A situation partly integrated, partly segregated, however, must remain neither fully rational nor fully agreeable.

The difference between independence and freedom, or between liberation and emancipation, makes every relationship between Negroes and whites, or between Jews and Gentiles, irretrievably complicated. When people are opposed and apart their problems are far simpler than the problems of people opposed and together. Could any man in his right senses expect the intricate problems of a child-parent relationship to be rationally resolved—let us say, by a contractual settlement? No more can there be a reasonable, amicable, and conclusive settlement of the problematic relationship between the emancipated and their emancipators, when partial integration and not full independence is the goal.

The history of Jewish emancipation should have taught us not to expect any clean and rational solution of the problem of Negro integration. The methods of the current black militancy, in spite of appearances, can only achieve a status as indecisive as that of the permanently institutionalized Jewish minority, on however different a basis. The Negroes are employing political pressures and mass action in a way totally foreign to American Jews, but what they look like they are accomplishing is no nearer to complete absorption.

Their aim is to break out of the subordinate social and economic roles institutionally assigned to them by local law, custom, or the de facto consequences of their history. Their method, autonomous ethnic organization and mass political pressures, may well force significant breakthroughs in the barriers that confine them. Jobs at the bottom, unskilled or skilled, which are not being left to them fast enough by the upward social mobility of white laborers will, no doubt, be opened up at a faster rate by effective pressure, in spite of backlash from middle-American ethnic groups. Trade unions, unable to freeze the present arrangements, will, perhaps, facilitate the preferential intake of the ghetto *Lumpenproletariat* into such positions. Economic functions in the ghetto not yet given up in the face of riots, boycotts, and instruments of black community organization and control may be increasingly abandoned by Jews and other whites; and the potential Negro economy this might make available might mature at a faster rate if black nationalism could implant the will and need for achievement widely in the community. Under pressure of militant tactics more and more blacks may be moved through the systems of education; and methods of preference may help them flow increasingly into the zone of expanding science-related industries of the economy at large.

Taking all these possibilities at the most optimistic estimates, it is obvious that the chances nevertheless favor the persistence of a black *Lumpenproletariat* of disproportionate size. Their pressure, already actively exerted to this end, may help force sweeping extensions of welfare state policies. Negative income taxes and guaranteed minimum incomes; radical broadening of the scope of free public education, medical care, and subsidized housing: these and other programs of support for the consumer

187

at the expense of the taxpayer may well be achieved soon. (The support of the Jewish vote is certainly to be counted on.) Without an intermediate socialist phase of public ownership of the means of production, capitalist America may move well into a quasicommunist stage, granting to each out of public resources a good part of what he thinks he needs. But the *Lumpenproletariat* whose pressure would have helped decisively in these advances would still remain a distinct, subordinate social stratum of the real America.

None of these imagined developments exhausts the full revolutionary potential for the black masses were the ghetto *Lumpenproletariat* to be seriously and systematically organized and used as the social base of revolution. One of the lessons of our time is how easy it is to cripple an advanced sophisticated civilization. If all the discontented customers of one of our large public utilities in a large city should turn on their complex electric appliances simultaneously at a given moment, by that simple act alone they might cause a power failure that could paralyze a major industrial region. In Boston not long ago a few score angry citizens, protesting the local airport authority's intended land seizures, tied up the whole town by the simple, legal expedient of driving through vehicular tunnels in column at a slow pace. Small groups of violent men have shown time and again how to collapse great structures of social organization, at least temporarily, by well-placed applications of force. Certainly, if the whole resentment of the black mass were mobilized and systematically applied to strategic sabotage, obstruction, and general wrecking, those in command of this force might reasonably hope, in the proper circumstances, to accomplish a revolution.

There are those in the black community, like the Black Panthers, who seem willing to take this road. So long as they voice these views sporadically, polemically, and act on them in the context of immediate local provocations, they enjoy the sympathy of Negroes generally and are protected by its solidarity. The more it begins to seem that they would really make the black mass a tool of general revolution, the greater the opposition of other Negroes. There is a very lively and very well-justified suspicion in the ghettos of anyone who would make Negroes catspaws to snatch white victories out of the fire of white quarrels. So long as the Black Panthers make white radicals—notably, Jewish radicals—blindly accept black demands, their battles with the police make them ghetto heroes, in spite of their white associates. But if the Black Panthers should go far enough in their united front tactics to look like pink assimilationists (as they begin to do when they unite with drug cultists and far-out women's liberationists and the Gay Liberation) the day of their popularity would turn to dusk.

One might add that the very success of the Negro militancy in consolidating the community signals the dialectical close of its revolutionary era, together with its revolutionary ethos. Some of the intellectuals and black bourgeois leaders restored to their own community will become its legitimate leaders; and should they ultimately conclude that the *Lumpenproletariat* tacticians are selling the community out to a revolutionary united front against the ethnic interests of blacks, they will turn against them without hesitation. In such a confrontation, the integrationist leaders may well win a decisive victory, and in any case make the black mass unavailable as a ready tool of revolutionary adventurers.

The net effect of black revolutionary militancy may then be to enhance dialectically the partial integration of the Negro masses. There are inherent flaws and faults and disagreeable side-effects of this outcome, however, which will constitute the continuing Negro problem of the future, as they do the contemporary American Jewish problem.

The Negro community may not be aware of it—though I think it is—but there is a pervasive tone of envy in the observations

189

young Jewish intellectuals make today concerning the current Negro revolution. Remembering the exhilarating days of Jewish radicalism in the Thirties or the fight for Israel in the Forties —remembering this if one lived it, or thinking back to it if one was too young and had missed it—Jews are tempted to say that never again, after they shall indeed have overcome, will Negroes have it as good. When oppression will have vanished, when Negroes in their due proportion will sit on the board of directors of AT&T and General Motors, when the universities and trade unions and the county courthouses in the Deep South together with the suburban country clubs in the North will be proportionately populated by every race as well as creed—on that glad day, will the Negro morale still be as high? Will the intellectual and the teenage dropout still be as much at one? Will the Negro professional still feel accountable to the laborer, the storekeeper, and the slumdweller?

What values will then hold them together in effective solidarity? The present Negro rebellion supplies a potent myth to serve as an ideological principle upon which the Negro community can build its separation. When the Negroes will have won the aims of their present struggle, in the manner and degree this proves possible, the values of sheer rebellion will be much less basic in their consensus. Hostility, which is always one aspect of the consensus of a suppressed subcommunity, cannot serve as the whole passive consensus that holds a group together; or it can only do so in the passing heat of active conflict. Culture, the lasting deposit of memorable moments of a people's experience, can build memories of the heroism and sense of freedom of the rebellion into a free community's basic consensus, but sheer hostility can only hold it together so long as it is unfree.

The more successful the Negro rebellion the more obvious this will become. Martin Luther King, Malcolm X, and other memorials of the current struggle will certainly be valued by

Negroes in a way no others can fully share; but the very reverse of the values of rebellion will have to be built into the institutions of their subculture and subcommunity. They will adapt in their own style not only general Christian values and general American status symbols but general middle class values as well.

The result of such a development might be that the Negro subcommunity would be totally absorbed; but this is unlikely. It is far more probable that integration will remain partial. The closer to equality the Negro community then comes, the more it will absorb the middle class style of general American and Christian values, the more prestige will accrue to its own conventional leadership, and the more effectively they will control the independent Negro consensus. The critical political and social problems of the Negro position in America may be contained or reduced in this way. But the Negro community might then highlight in previously unmatched clarity another American problem of which they are already the prime example. How can an American subcommunity which exists by force of circumstance alone justify its separate existence unless it is something more than a separate though equal replica of all the rest of America? How can it sustain its elan and solidarity, or even keep up a satisfactory morale and provide an adequate focus for identification?

A Jew who has gone this route to a high level of partial absorption, and who knows with willing acceptance or with resignation that he will not travel the road of assimilation to the end, knows too the answers to some of these questions. With advancing integration comes creeping deterioration of the morale and solidarity of the segregated group. These qualities of the militant minority are not only admirable but badly needed when this road has been traveled to the halfway point at which the journey must and should be suspended.

The highly adjusted and integrated minority remains embattled in America. The stakes are now its own secure identity.